CAPACITY BUILDING FOR SCHOOL I

CONTEMPORARY APPROACHES TO RESEARCH IN LEARNING INNOVATIONS

Volume 6

Rationale:
Learning today is no longer confined to schools and classrooms. Modern information and communication technologies make the learning possible any where, any time. The emerging and evolving technologies are creating a knowledge era, changing the educational landscape, and facilitating the learning innovations. In recent years educators find ways to cultivate curiosity, nurture creativity and engage the mind of the learners by using innovative approaches.

Contemporary Approaches to Research in Learning Innovations explores approaches to research in learning innovations from the learning sciences view. Learning sciences is an interdisciplinary field that draws on multiple theoretical perspectives and research with the goal of advancing knowledge about how people learn. The field includes cognitive science, educational psychology, anthropology, computer and information science and explore pedagogical, technological, sociological and psychological aspects of human learning. Research in this approaches examine the social, organizational and cultural dynamics of learning environments, construct scientific models of cognitive development, and conduct design-based experiments.

Contemporary Approaches to Research in Learning Innovations covers research in developed and developing countries and scalable projects which will benefit everyday learning and universal education. Recent research includes improving social presence and interaction in collaborative learning, using epistemic games to foster new learning, and pedagogy and praxis of ICT integration in school curricula.

Capacity Building for School Improvement

Revisited

By

Patricia Stringer

SENSE PUBLISHERS
ROTTERDAM / BOSTON / TAIPEI

A C.I.P. record for this book is available from the Library of Congress.

ISBN 978-94-6209-327-0 (paperback)
ISBN 978-94-6209-328-7 (hardback)
ISBN 978-94-6209-329-4 (e-book)

Published by: Sense Publishers,
P.O. Box 21858, 3001 AW Rotterdam, The Netherlands
https://www.sensepublishers.com/

Printed on acid-free paper

CONTENTS

CONTENTS

CONTENTS

LIST OF FIGURES

ACKNOWLEDGEMENTS

When I gave serious consideration to writing this book, the school which was at the centre of this research on capacity building for school improvement became the focus. I was part of this school's journey towards improvement both prior to and during the research process. This gave me the much needed insight to construct the model on capacity building for school improvement portrayed in this book. Recording the journey this group of school stakeholders took towards improving their school meant that I am able to share their practices on capacity building with educators from around the world. The book captures this school's journey from the viewpoint of attributes, practices and themes that underpin capacity building. Working with this school's stakeholders has been a privilege, not just for the insights they gave me on building capacity for school improvement, and why, but also for the opportunity to meet, talk and pursue their views on improvement aligned to improving outcomes for students. This book is very much their story. With this in mind, my grateful thanks are extended to all stakeholders who have generously welcomed me into their school, made time to talk to me and allowed me to observe their practices. To the most committed and dedicated educators I have had the good fortune to meet, I wish to express my deepest thanks.

I wish to thank Dr. Myint Swe Khine, associate professor and head of Science, Mathematics and ICT Academic Group at Bahrain Teachers College who encouraged me to write this book. I'm not sure how these things work out but I suspect that talking to Myint set off a chain of reactions that culminated in the writing of this book.

I wish to thank my colleagues for their encouragement and support. In particular, my sincere thanks to Samia who helped in the formatting of this book.

Finally, I dedicate this book to my family who have always supported me. I would like to thank my mum Doris for her encouragement. I would like to thank my husband Geoff who contributed significantly to this effort in his own talented way. I also want to thank my son John for his contributions and for all that he does by way of support.

ABOUT THE AUTHOR

Patricia Stringer received her Bachelor of Arts degree from Auckland University and her Master of Education Administration and Education Doctorate degrees at Massey University Auckland, New Zealand. She has had over 25 years of teaching experience in the New Zealand primary school and tertiary sector. As a senior manager in several schools, she has had the privilege of working alongside principals, education authorities and community groups initiating school improvement. She has had first-hand experience in turning around a school categorised as 'failing'. In her educational advisory capacity, she worked with schools implementing *The New Zealand Curriculum Framework*. Her professional background extends to lecturing in graduate and post graduate courses at the Faculty of Education, University of Auckland, Auckland College of Education and Massey University. Patricia is currently working in a tertiary institution in the Middle East as assistant professor, head of education studies and curriculum coordinator.

INTRODUCTION

Throughout my career I have been fascinated with the notion of reform and the drive to improve schools. I have witnessed successive waves of government reform policies initiate responses to act and change systems, processes and structures. The notion of school improvement is captivating. I ask myself how practitioners embrace and pursue improvement. How do they manage the inevitability of change that follows? Additional questions pertain to sustaining the improvement drive given the daily demands of life in schools. Progressively my thoughts are drawn towards understanding what happens in school environments that create and sustain an improvement culture. I find myself drawn to an examination of practice and, in this respect, the building of capacity for improvement.

Understanding the concept of capacity building for school improvement has held my attention for nearly two decades. Indeed, as a senior manager of various primary schools, I have often found myself at the centre of not only initiating change for improvement but, also, reflecting and questioning if improvements have become embedded and form part of 'how things are done around here'. My reflections in this regard focus on school systems, processes and structures that allow for effective introduction, implementation and sustainment of improvement measures in practice. My thoughts also extend to members of the school community who act as catalysts for change. As change agents, what do their actions involve? I am forever mindful that internal and external determinants of context influence practice and strategies employed to initiate, manage and sustain change over time. Questions and thoughts such as these motivated me to undertake research in the area of capacity building for school improvement. I felt compelled to undertake this study in a school categorised as 'underperforming'. Schools in such environments have compounding issues and challenges to deal with over and above the improvement journey. The case study school to which I will refer and draw examples from has, over a two year period, successfully implemented capacity building strategies which enabled its shift from being labelled 'underperforming' to having attained a remarkable turnaround for the better.

My association with the school in question has been progressive extending over a period of 7 years. In October 2001, I received an invitation to attend the newly appointed principal's powhiri.[i] In June 2002, I received an invitation to attend an advisory meeting with Ministry of Education officials, outside agency representatives,[ii] cluster school principals and school staff to brainstorm ideas on improvement that could draw a halt to and reverse a dysfunctional school ethos prevalent at the time. At this meeting, barriers to school change were identified and action plans for improvement discussed. Barriers included a negative school culture, low student academic levels, non-productive (verging on violent) in and out of class student behaviour, and community and property issues such as vandalism and dilapidated environmental conditions. Combined, these factors generated a negative school image, falling roll and low staff morale.

1

In January 2003, I received a further invitation to attend a 'teachers only' professional development day where action plans to counteract academic, behavioural and environmental concerns were discussed. At the meeting, opportunities to review progress made since the arrival of the new principal were undertaken. Information revealed that the school had initiated system and structural changes which were making a positive difference to student learning. Ministry officials and outside agency representatives acknowledged site-based factors leading to improvements in pedagogy and student behaviour.

By mid-2003, the school showed signs of being a *moving*[iii] school (Stoll & Fink, 1996). It displayed: a strong drive for organisational change based on the school's vision; professional leadership exercised at all levels and by different stakeholders; an emphasis on improving student academic achievement, teaching and learning; a supportive school culture; and continuous professional development for all stakeholders. It was at this time that I approached the school authorities – the principal and board of trustees[iv] – and sought their permission to conduct a study on how this school built its capacity to improve.

PURPOSE AND FOCUS

The purpose of this book is to help promote an understanding of attributes, practices and themes related to capacity building for school improvement. Many questions related to this phenomenon have, as yet, gone unanswered or unexplained by the literature. This book examines capacity building for school improvement at the level of practice where school stakeholders[v] craft and sustain the improvement process. Using this school as a case in point, the book explains, describes and analyses the following:
- Capacity building embedded in external (macro) and internal (micro) contexts of reform and change;
- Attributes and practices which underpin the phenomenon; and
- Attributes, practices and emerging themes that contribute to a model of capacity building for school improvement.

The book addresses concerns and questions related to capacity building as seen through the eyes of a variety of school stakeholders: the principal; senior managers; teachers; auxiliary staff; and parents directly engaged in improvement efforts. In practice, it determines and makes recommendations on what policy makers, reform developers and school stakeholders can do to enhance the building of capacity for improvement. The book features vignettes that exemplify successful practice. Recommendations, summarised in Chapter 10, may be of assistance in future development of policies and policy implementation measures that build capacity for school improvement.

CHANGE AND LINKS TO CAPACITY BUILDING

The future ain't what it used to be. (Yogi Berra, 2001)

In response to this statement, Smylie (2010) notes the preponderance of three arguments related to improving schools and schooling. First, these are rapidly changing and unpredictable times and with a future characterised by rapid change, systemic uncertainty and even chaos, schools appear unprepared. Smylie notes, "Most of today's schools are yesterday schools built for purposes and contexts disappearing or gone. They are oriented toward the past not the future" (p. 2). Second, schools are built to promote stability and to be stable. They do not change on their own nor are they easily changed by others. Third, schools must change in basic ways to perform effectively in the future. "They must become more flexible and adaptable, better able to deal with increasing complexity and ambiguity, more proactive than reactive and reoriented towards different objectives" (ibid.). All three arguments purport a call for change that is future orientated and which builds capacity for improvement. This call may mean that existing norms, structures and processes need replacing to establish 'fit' with an evolving school ethos and the values and ethical purposes symbolic of context. Reframing what happens in schools requires school authorities, outside agencies and government officials working together in new ways to achieve: meaningful communication across all levels of schooling; appropriate capacity building practices; problem solving mindsets; and leadership that initiates, manages and sustains change. The call to build capacity seems central to any debate on school improvement and emphasised is the need to combine internal and external agendas in initiating and implementing change (Day, 2007). Accompanying this is the urgency for action underpinned by clear theory (Harris, 2010).

Capacity building is, by its very nature, a public enterprise to which many definitions are accorded. Mitchell and Sackney (2000) state capacity building results from single-loop and double-loop learning. Single-loop learning occurs within existing structural arrangements influenced by a shared organisational memory of prior events and existing ways of knowing (Marks & Louis, 1999). Double-loop learning generates new rather than adaptive learning by collaboratively examining the root causes of issues and questioning the basic assumptions that underlie existing professional attitudes and behaviours (Senge 2000). Over time, double-loop learning builds up sufficient personal and interpersonal capacities to sustain a mutually accountable community of learners where shared norms and values focus on student learning, reflective dialogue, de-privatisation of practice and collaboration. Darling Hammond (1996) notes that such a shift represents a move away from enforcing procedures to building capacity and from managing compliance to managing improvement.

In a study on primary schools in Wales by Harris (2010), the notion of collective capacity building was emphasised. Collective capacity building relates to 'interdependent practice' (Sharrat & Fullan, 2009) explained as collaboration of professionals within schools and across local authorities with the purpose of

3

transforming learning and teaching. Harris (2010) claims this encourages the development of professional learning communities with potential to improve and raise student performance. Although professional learning communities are powerful vehicles for change, detailed studies of how this occurs in practice are not well represented in the literature (Giles, 2007).

ORGANISATION

This book presents a model of capacity building for school improvement grounded in everyday practice. It highlights organisational attributes and capacity building practices that facilitate improvement. Though patterns may vary across schools, the attributes, practices and themes identified in this book based on a case study of one school are considered applicable to other sites. Taken together, attributes, practices and themes provide a sound basis to discuss the hallmarks of a model on capacity building for school improvement.

Chapter 1 sets the scene. It sheds light on the challenges of implementing and sustaining capacity given an evolving, rapidly changing educational landscape. The focus of this chapter on the New Zealand educational scene provides an overview of government reform policies designed to promote improvement. Against this backdrop, hidden paradoxes inherent in policy and policy implementation measures are discussed from the viewpoint of what builds and, simultaneously, detracts from capacity building for school improvement. This chapter proceeds to define components of the capacity building for school improvement model which is subsequently unpacked in the chapters that follow.

Chapters 2 to 5 draw attention to attributes underpinning the phenomenon. Here, the importance of vision, stakeholders as change agents, school culture and professional development are highlighted and explained. The discussion of each attribute is embedded in an improving school context with established links to practice. Chapter 2 highlights the importance of vision as providing the blueprint or map for all capacity building for school improvement efforts. Chapter 3 considers the importance of stakeholders as change agents in building capacity. Chapter 4 highlights important cultural hallmarks of a school's culture that provides a suitable environment from which to build capacity. Chapter 5 details the importance of professional development that leads to professional learning considered an important contributor to practices that build capacity for improvement.

The next three chapters, Chapters 6, 7 and 8, identify and discuss key practices inherent in capacity building. Practices identified are: knowledge production and utilisation, a 'switching on' mentality and division of labour: roles and responsibilities. Key characteristics of each are explained in relation to what happens in this setting connected to capacity building. Actions of school stakeholders are highlighted. Chapter 6 argues that processes for knowledge production and utilisation are critical in creating a learning culture, improving pedagogy and lifting outcomes for students. Chapter 7 captures the notion of a 'switching on' mentality as a motivational force driving change for improvement.

Chapter 8 explains the roles and responsibilities school stakeholders play in building capacity for improvement. Of concern is division of labour: roles and responsibilities.

In Chapter 9, the theoretical framework that explains capacity building for school improvement is explicated utilising the four themes of situated activity; connectedness; governance, leadership and management; and capacity outcomes. The theoretical model draws on attributes and practices previously discussed.

The final chapter, Chapter 10, reflects on policy/practice related implications highlighted by the study. It presents recommendations for policy makers and school personnel that can be used as a guide to maximise efforts in the building of capacity for improvement.

NOTES

[i] A powhiri is a Maori welcoming ceremony involving speeches, dancing, singing and finally the hongi (pressing one's nose and forehead with that of another person during an encounter) Retrieved from: www.en.wikipedia.org/wiki/Powhiri.

[ii] Outside agency representatives can refer to one of many groups of people involved in school support.

[iii] Rosenholt's (1989) explains that the 'moving' school displays positive work conditions and produces much higher outcomes for students. Hopkins, Ainscow and West (1994) note the moving school displays "a healthy balance of change and stability, and balanced development and maintenance ... as it adapts successfully to an often rapidly changing environment" (p. 91).

[iv] All New Zealand's state and state-integrated schools have a board of trustees. The board of trustees is the Crown entity responsible for the governance and the control of the management of the school. The board is the employer of all staff in the school, is responsible for setting the school's strategic direction in consultation with parents, staff and students, and ensuring that its school provides a safe environment and quality education for all its students. Boards are also responsible for overseeing the management of personnel, curriculum, property, finance and administration. Trustees are elected by the parent community, staff members and, in the case of schools with students above Year 9, the students. The principal is also a board member. Retrieved from: www.educationcounts.govt.nz/data-services/data-collections/boards_of_trustees.

[v] School stakeholders in this case includes: the principal, senior managers, teachers, auxiliary staff, and parents.

SETTING THE STAGE

An examination of practice with a view to improve it necessitates a consideration of context within which the interplay of external (macro) and internal (micro) determinants account for particular site-based characteristics. From a position of understanding context, it is possible to determine not only type and trajectory of improvement needed but, also, capacity building attributes and practices unique to the site that works towards it. This chapter begins with a brief review of the New Zealand government's reform policies by way of providing a contextual backdrop within which to raise the argument that reform policies are simultaneously responsible for generating and limiting efforts to build capacity. Government policies not only affect the direction school improvement takes but, also, its trajectory. Establishing 'fit' within externally imposed government policy and internal determinants of context is what drives a school to construct its own unique brand of what it means to improve and build capacity. In this chapter, capacity building and school improvement terms are defined in relation to contemporary literature and findings from this study. Hidden paradoxes embedded in government policy are discussed. The model for capacity building is introduced in this chapter and deconstructed in the chapters that follow.

REFORMS LINKED TO CAPACITY BUILDING AND SCHOOL IMPROVEMENT

In New Zealand, much emphasis has and continues to be directed towards school improvement in pursuit of raising student achievement and reducing disparity (Ministry of Education, 1999a, 2004; Alton-Lee, 2003). Over the last decade, action in this area is traceable to key policy statements. The 1999 briefing paper, for example, prepared for the incoming Minister of Education by the Ministry of Education (MOE) stressed the importance of increasing achievement levels and reducing disparity to enhance New Zealand's social and economic well-being and adaptation to growing international and technological influences, ethnic diversity and calls for lifelong education (MOE, 1999a). The Ministry of Education's first Statement of Intent for the period 2003-2008 promoted education as a lifelong process to keep pace with a changing world (MOE, 2004). Underpinning elements emphasised: the need to be more responsive to diverse cultures and a wide range of needs and aspirations; globalisation; the impact of technology and information; and development of a knowledge-based economy. To ensure this, high standards and clear expectations at all levels in the education system were stressed. Attention was given to developing a schools' sector strategy focused on raising achievement and reducing disparity. Implied in the Statement of Intent was the Ministry's involvement to influence and improve system-wide learning outcomes from a substantial knowledge-base and increased systems capabilities. In the Statement of Intent 2005-2010, the Ministry reasserted its mission of raising achievement and reducing disparity (MOE, 2006). Three outcomes to be covered were: effective teaching for all students; family and community engagement in education; and development of quality providers. To ensure these overarching goals were met, a wide range of legislative mandates, official documentation and research were promoted. Mandates contained in *The National Education Guidelines*[vi] (MOE, 1993a) and *The New Zealand Curriculum Framework* (1993b) indicated commitment to improving schools. Changes to *The National Administration Guidelines* (NAGs) (MOE, 1993a) and the 2001 amendment to the 1989 Education Act placed planning for and reporting on student achievement at the top of schools' agendas. The amendments legislated that schools' charters must indicate plans for ongoing improvement (MOE, 2000). Legislative changes to governance roles increased board responsibility in monitoring student achievement and reviewing effectiveness of teaching and learning in relation to expectations set by the school. Work undertaken by the Ministry included building relationships with other educational agencies[vii] to ensure system coherence and develop interagency cooperation and integration in implementing strategies, activities and services that promote better outcomes for students (MOE, 2004). The focus was on addressing the needs of at-risk children, young people and families; providing second-chance opportunities; building a knowledge base; and working with agencies to ensure pastoral and health needs of learners were supported (MOE, 2004).

Government goals, strategies and Ministry outcomes have seen a range of projects initiated to raise school effectiveness, enhance professional capabilities of educators and support student learning. The following are a few examples of Ministry (Research Division) projects under the headings of Assessment, Curriculum, Schools, and Special Needs:

− Assessment: Assessment Resource Banks for Classroom Teachers; National Education Monitoring Project; Programme for International Student Achievement 2006 (PISA-06) − Third Cycle; Science Study 2006/2007 (TIMSS-06/07)
− Curriculum: Monitoring of Reading Recovery Data; Resource Teachers of Literacy: Annual Monitoring; Evaluation of the professional development strategy to improve literacy in secondary schools
− Schools: A study of Students' Transition from Primary to Secondary Schooling
− Special Needs: Enhanced Programme Funding (EPF) Evaluation.

The Ministry of Education with teacher unions, educational leaders, researchers and teacher educators has been proactive in managing the development of a series of Best Evidence Synthesis (BES) reports that exemplify the practice of teachers.[viii] The purpose is to develop a, "shared, constantly updated knowledge base to inform dialogue and improve the work of teacher educators, practitioners, researchers and policy development" (Alton-Lee, 2005, pp. 6-7). Alton-Lee claims that this approach to effect improvement is not about prescribing practice from the past but drawing out, "principles and characteristics underpinning effective practice in recognition of the importance of context and the complexity and creativity of any teaching endeavour" (ibid., p. 7). In addition to the BES reports, Ministry convened reviews inform evaluations of certain programmes and these have added to an increasing knowledge base focused on improving schools.

Supplementing the Ministry of Education's national knowledge base, the Education Review Office (ERO)[ix] provides reviews on schools and early childhood providers and national and cluster reports. Reviews are public documents available from ERO or downloaded from their web site (ERO, 2006a). National and cluster reports are also easily accessible, designed to give parents, boards of trustees, teachers, government officials and other interested parties information on improvement and opportunities for debate on what counts as quality in education policy and practice.

Such evidence confirms a national push to raise achievement levels and reduce disparity with focused attention on school improvement. Despite this mass of legislation, policies and research, challenges persist and affect what it means to improve schools and build capacity for improvement. In this chapter I start by defining school improvement and capacity building. Following this, I will discuss macro level government policies traceable to the initiation of *Tomorrow's Schools* in lieu of tensions and implications for school stakeholders involved in building capacity for improvement.

SCHOOL IMPROVEMENT AND CAPACITY BUILDING: TERMS DEFINED

The New Zealand Curriculum Framework (1993) and various curriculum documents link school improvement to social, academic and cognitive growth and development of students. School improvement is, however, a complex and difficult concept to define in simple terms as it is constantly evolving with differentiated calls for action over time (Potter, Reynolds, & Chapman, 2002).

The late 1970's to early 1980s, exemplified by the OECD's *International School Improvement Project* (ISIP) (Hopkins, 1987), defined school improvement as, "systematic, sustained effort aimed at change in learning conditions and other related internal conditions in one or more schools, with the ultimate aim of accomplishing educational goals more effectively" (van Valzen et al., 1985, p. 48). Although careful planning, management and implementation were emphasised, many initiatives of the period were, "free floating, rather than representing a systematic, programmatic and coherent approach to school change ..." (Potter, Reynolds, & Chapman, 2002, p. 244). Organisational change, school self-evaluation and stakeholder 'buy-in' (Fullan, 1991) were loosely connected to student learning outcomes (Potter, Reynolds, & Chapman, 2002) and had little impact on classroom practice (Reynolds, 1999; Hopkins, 2001).

The early 1990s heralded support for a merged school improvement and effectiveness perspective (Reynolds, Hopkins, & Stoll, 1993). School effectiveness was said to contribute value-added methodologies for judging and explaining what works to raise student achievement (Teddlie & Reynolds, 2000). School improvement was defined as a, "distinct approach to educational change that enhances student achievement as well as strengthening the school's capacity for managing change seriously" (Hopkins, Ainscow, & West, 1994, p. 3). In an era of burgeoning decentralisation, inclusion of the term 'capacity' called for: self-management, taking charge of change, developing ownership, setting own directions and adapting mandates to fit organisational vision. In reality, Barth (1990) notes such arguments proved unconvincing and presented an oversimplified picture which Hopkins, Beresford and West (1998) caution, "tells us little about how one affects the other" (p. 116).

Over the last five or six years, researchers have relied on findings from large scale projects to define improvement. Such projects include: *Improving the Quality of Education for All* (IQEA) in England, *The Manitoba School Improvement* (MSIP) in Canada and *Success For All* (SFA) in the United States. IQEA, MSIP and SFA projects maintain a focus on what happens in classrooms and the importance of learning. The emphasis is on specifying learning outcomes rather than general learning goals. There is clear articulation of an instructional framework that guides developmental activity and provides teachers with a shared pedagogical focus to try new strategies and share new experiences. In all projects, teacher professional development and professional learning communities are given high priority. The importance of reflection is emphasised. Providing teachers with opportunities to work together and enquire into pedagogical practice is seen to foster positive collegial relationships, shared values, norms, agreed goals, group trust and respect. Underlying principles and practices from all projects prove particularly relevant in defining school improvement as it currently exists. Indeed, findings from the case study school confirm that aforementioned principles and practices are crucial in establishing a culture within which capacity building for improvement can flourish.

A review of contemporary New Zealand research also confirms a focus on organisational and pedagogical change to advance school improvement. In the New Zealand study *Sustaining school improvement: Ten primary school's journeys* (2002), Mitchell, Cameron and Wylie identify three approaches. First, school improvement as 'development' adopts an institutional perspective generated by those in schools within local contexts, relationships and national and international frameworks. Improvement is defined as a continuous and evolving process, 'the way things are around here' (Mitchell et al., 2002). Schools are considered learning communities with active stakeholder engagement in learning and problem-solving. Second, school improvement as lifting performance is endorsed mainly by Ministry of Education and Treasury officials (Mitchell et al., 2002). Government assistance is linked to policy interventions in support of change and provision of safety net mechanisms to assist individual at risk schools meet their legal obligations – a more serious intervention. The role of school culture, values, needs analysis and goals continue to be emphasised as fundamental to any change attempt. Improvement through external incentives (Mitchell et al., 2002), the third approach, emphasises meeting national or international academic standards within a competitive setting. In today's climate of neo liberalism, this discourse appears unavoidable; part of the educational landscape schools and school leaders confront daily.

No singular definition aptly captures school improvement. As a social construct, it is time and context specific which leads researchers such as Annan, Faamoe-Timoteo, Carpenter, Hucker and Warren (2004) to suggest that, "A one-size fits all approach to schooling improvement is not going to cater for the development needs of all schools" (p. 36). Regardless of definition type, factors that lead to improvement are identifiable and McCauley and Roddick (2001) in *An Evaluation of Schools Support*, identify the following:

– Identification of shared goals and strategies based on a thorough needs analysis and ongoing development and renewal cycle;
– Establishment of external connections for expertise and guidance;
– Development of strong school-wide leadership;
– Expansion of teachers' knowledge in and use of student achievement data to improve teaching and learning; and
– Change that occurs at multiple levels within a school.

The term capacity building implies a deeper understanding of school change, more than, "just translating school level characteristics into 'doing words'" (Hopkins et al., 1998, p. 117). Maden (2001) notes capacity is, "the single most important matter in trying to identify how and why some schools maintain and sustain improvement" (p. 320). Fullan (2005) describes the concept as, "developing the collective ability – dispositions, skills, knowledge, motivation, and resources – to act together to bring about positive change" (p. 4). Stoll, Bolman, McMahon, Wallace and Thomas (2006) suggest the concept links best to sustainable school improvement achieved in professional learning communities. Professional learning communities is defined as a group of people sharing and evaluating practice in ongoing, reflective, collaborative, inclusive and learning-oriented ways.

An expanded perspective of school capacity building, as advanced by Goodman, Baron and Myers (2005), relates to building community capacity. Based on empowerment or enhancement theory, these authors advocate that parents can change conditions provided they have access to appropriate knowledge. In this respect, productive home-school partnerships are linked to school improvement. Underpinning reasons for this, as purported by Gold, Simon and Brown (2005), suggest parent communities with self-efficacy are better able to combat the demands placed on them by those in positions of power; parents capacity adds value and sustains the school's vision and momentum for change over time; and community capacity creates political will that motivates officials to take action. In an era of decentralisation and self-managing schools, such arguments hold appeal. However, research in this area is limited and the literature that is available pursues a rather narrow conception of parental involvement in, for example, voluntary assistance (Driscoll & Goldring, 2005).

Any inquiry into capacity building must consider factors that negate and/or serve as limitations to the improvement process. In this regard, Hadfield, Chapman, Curryer and Barrett in *Building Capacity Developing Your School* (2004) identify the following:

- Improvement policies with unrealistic expectations and pressures that damage chances of sustaining improvement by mismanaging the external environment;
- Inability to sustain individual development over longer periods;
- Lack of a common language around teaching and learning; and
- Challenges surrounding traditional notions of leadership versus delegated responsibilities. Findings from Hadfield et al.'s study suggest that leadership which is less hierarchical and traditional is more suited to building capacity.

Capacity building, like school improvement, is difficult to conceptualise and generalise. The results from this study indicate that it is a process embedded in context and with an ever present fragility especially if processes that account for its initial conception are ill-conceived. They also suggest that external (macro) and internal (micro) factors are influential determinants. In this book, I suggest that capacity building for improvement is a response to meeting individual, collective and systemic needs so as to maintain school equilibrium while pursuing advancement in the direction of improvement. The focus must be on lifting outcomes for students. The concept is time and context dependent.

ISSUES AFFECTING CAPACITY BUILDING FOR SCHOOL IMPROVEMENT

Many issues of an external, macro political nature present themselves as challenges affecting the school improvement and capacity building process. Like many OECD countries, New Zealand has encountered public service reform driven by economic rationalism (Dalin, 2005). As Dalin (2005) notes, "Programmes are being introduced that seek to decentralise services, simplify regulations, and develop expertise and new management" (p. 4). In New Zealand, privatisation of schools, democratisation of school systems, enhanced parent participation and administrative and financial reforms were designed to: increase system productivity by devolving ownership to those closest to the action, increase democratic decision making by situating processes closer to service users and increase relevance and quality of educational delivery by ensuring, "*well-informed, well-educated and experienced teachers draw on theory and practice to reflect over the dilemmas of teaching*" (Dalin, 2005, p. 22, italics in the original). Such changes in the political scene exert powerful influences on what happens in schools. In this chapter, I examine New Zealand's neo-liberal reforms of the 1990's from the viewpoint of recurring tensions, constraints and opportunities schools and school leaders' face in building capacity for improvement. Furthermore, I suggest that variations of school contexts impose their own unique challenges which suggest a differentiated, situated take on capacity building and school improvement.

Neo-liberal Reforms of the 1990s in New Zealand

Changes heralded by the *Tomorrow's Schools* policy (Lange, 1988) placed administration of education in New Zealand, "within the orbit of economic policy" (Codd, 2005, p. 193). Prior to *Tomorrow's Schools*, New Zealand's education system was dominated by a Keynesian progressive-liberal ideology which Boyd (1998) suggests, served three main functions: integrative (integration of youth into mainstream society), egalitarian (equalisation of the skills gap and reduction of extremes of wealth and poverty) and developmental (personal and moral development). The 1990s saw this liberal democratic ideology subsumed by neo-liberal ideas advancing individual freedom and choice through market forces where "the market becomes the regulatory mechanism, and government intervention can be reduced to a minimum" (Boyd, 1998, p. 5). Calls for reforms were backed by arguments that, "parents, teachers, students and local communities (needed) more say in educational decision making and school government" (Barrington, 1981, p. 68) and, "instead of uniformity there may be an appropriate diversity, reflecting variations in local needs and circumstances" (p. 68).

Tomorrow's Schools policies were claimed to be a response to alleviate heavily centralised, rule-bound, inflexible, central and regional administrative structures (Dalin, 2005), combined with worsening economic conditions (Codd, 2005; Dalin, 2005; Boyd, 1998; Whitty, Power & Haplin, 1998). They were also a reaction to assertions that schools were unresponsive to parental concerns (MOE, 2005). The Taskforce to Review Education Administration (*Administering for Excellence*, 1988) proposed increasing educational administration efficiency by decreasing government operational involvement in schools. This led to the 'direct resourcing experiment' (Whitty, Power & Haplin, 1998) initiated in 1988 to give school leaders freedom to respond to local community needs while satisfying government policy requirements for accountability (Leithwood, 2001) and efficiency (MOE, 2005). The policy promoted self-managing and self-governing schools charged with acting within legislative guidelines driven by an accountability-focused political framework (Leithwood, 2001).

The current situation that exists in New Zealand stipulates boards of trustees' governance over state and integrated schools. Boards are comprised of elected parents, the principal and a staff representative. Boards have legal authority for school governance and management (ERO, 1999). Each state school has its own distinctive charter based on *The National Educational Guidelines*. The charter, approved by the Ministry and signed by the Minister, is a contract between the school and the Ministry. It ensures compliance to government mandates. Regular school reviews conducted by ERO officials ensure board compliance to legislative guidelines. Governance is meant to be a reflective mix of democratic and managerial ideals aimed at increasing administrative efficiency and parental responsiveness in the way schools are run (MOE, 2005).

The situation that unfolded with the advent of *Tomorrow's Schools* has raised critique among educators. For example, Robinson, Ward, Timperley and Tuioti (2005) suggest that freedom to manage does not imply reduced accountability to the government. Rather, government priorities remain prominent but with a shift from accountability of inputs and procedures (money spent and processes employed) to outputs (services) and outcomes (results). They add that results-oriented accountability is difficult to achieve because boards of trustees' attention is continually diverted to compliance and legislative requirements, fiscal

13

responsibilities, health and safety matters and delivery of the curriculum. Further, self-managing schools, designed to increase efficiency, has proven inefficient in responding to local community needs; abolishment of enrolment zones has established a competitive market place in education; and site-based democratic school governance has induced school level bureaucracy (Thrupp & Willmott, 2003). Although there is acceptance of *Tomorrow's Schools* policies, a climate of paradoxes where ideas espoused seem to be at odds with one another continues to prevail. Tensions revolve around: encouragement of local decision-making but within strict legislative guidelines; high expectations of school improvement yet inadequate resourcing to successfully implement new innovations and parental involvement in governance/decision-making without thought of compromising professional autonomy (Dalin, 2005). The sections that follow elaborate on how tensions of funding, decentralisation and accountability, governance and low decile socio economic factors negate efforts to build capacity for improvement.

Funding

In a context of reform, funding is generally considered an essential contributor to school improvement. The situation that currently exists in New Zealand is that state and integrated schools receive an operations grant from the Ministry of Education calculated on student numbers. This operations grant covers every expense, excluding teaching staff salaries (except in the few schools that are fully funded). Schools are allocated further monies according to decile ranking: Targeted Funding for Educational Achievement (TFEA), Special Education Grant (SEG), Careers Information Grant (CIG) and Decile Discretionary Funding. Fundraising, school donations, foreign fee paying students and the like attract other monies. The argument voiced by proponents calling for a change in the funding formula (Codd, 2005; Hawk & Hill, 1997) suggest that this situation encourages interschool competition for students in educational environments best described as 'enterprise cultures' (Codd, 2005). As funding per school follows a pro-rata student enrolment formula, roll reduction leads to cutbacks of funds which negatively affect staffing, resources and teacher professional development. The 'ripple effect' created (Hargreaves & Fink, 2006) is said to impede the building of capacity for school improvement.

While much is said in support of funding to initiate change and improvement, an emerging body of empirical research (New Zealand and overseas) indicates that financial input has only marginal impact on improving the quality of classroom learning (Raudenbush, 2005). Annan, Fa'amoe-Timoteo, Carpenter, Hucker and Warren's (2004) report, *Strengthening Education in Mangere and Otara Outcomes Report July 1999-June 2002 A Three-Way Partnership to Raise Student Achievement*, points out that two schools in the *Strengthening Education in Mangere and Otara* (SEMO) project demonstrated improvement disconnected from additional government funding but related, instead, to strong professional and trustee leadership, effective supervision of classroom teaching and educational links among schools, staff and parents. Similar findings were reported by Earl and

Lee (1998) in their eight-year evaluation of a school improvement project in Manitoba. Findings from this study revealed little direct relationship between additional funding and success of individual schools. Rather, funding proved a catalyst for additional pressure and support. As an alternative, Earl and Lee identify the importance of a critical friend for ongoing knowledge and advice in the facilitation of school improvement. These findings offer an alternative perspective to the funding/school improvement debate and support Raudenbush's (2005) assertions that, "resources, by themselves, do not improve teaching and learning. Knowledge about how to use resources in instruction is the key, yet woefully lacking" and, "Given the current weakness in knowledge about how best to organise, coordinate, and enact effective instruction, it is hardly surprising that simply investing in new resources would have, at best, marginal effects on student outcomes" (p. 26).

Decentralisation and Accountability

Decentralisation that followed the launching of *Tomorrow's Schools* in New Zealand shifted accountability for student learning and school improvement from government to schools (Leithwood, 2001; Codd, 2005). Schools' ability to exercise flexibility, modify practice in line with community needs, democratise systems and build capacity was heralded as promoting improvement. However, as Dalin (2005), Robinson et al. (2005), Codd (2005), Rae (2005), Thrupp and Willmott (2003) and Thrupp (2001) note, transference of decision making from the state to schools is accompanied by strengthening government accountability over curriculum, assessment of learning and teaching and professional development. Freedom to manage does not imply reduced accountability (Robinson et al., 2005) rather, as Leithwood (2001) claims, it "increases administrators' accountability to the central district or board office for the efficient expenditure of resources" (p. 223). In addition, school leaders may not be well placed to deal with such huge task expectations; that is, success is heavily dependent on individual attributes that may be severely compromised in settings where a lack of knowledge, skills and experience of school personnel fail to promote professionalism or improvement. Compliance demands and calls for increased professionalism inform policies directed at raising teachers' and principals' competencies to "stay abreast of best professional practices" (Leithwood, 2001, p. 225). These add to complexities school leaders face in the quest for improvement. Self-management and lay governance, as the literature suggests, promote tensions that can, if not managed, negate efforts to build capacity for improvement.

Governance

In the years that have followed *Tomorrow's Schools*, a number of criticisms and challenges have been raised related to board performance in governance. The third and final ministerial evaluation report on SEMO, by Robinson et al. (2005), confirmed board ineffectiveness to three 'big' ideas the first of which revolved around definitions of 'governance'. Governance, by boards of trustees, was and to an extent continues to be considered a highly formalised activity with conformity to school-based and national policy requirements and guidelines (Robinson et al., 2005). Emphasis on formal positions of responsibilities and role demarcation of board members to perform tasks does not necessarily equate to shared understandings of role requirements. Indeed, Robinson et al. (2005) found conflicting views related to particular governance tasks. The commonly agreed notion was that 'good' governance equates to compliance and standardised ways of operating (Robinson et al., 2005) not critical inquiry of teaching and dialogue on ways to improve schools or build capacity.

Second, 'good' governance was understood as acting in accord with internalised understandings of what counts as good practice. However, as the report indicates, trustees:

> have little, if any, first hand experience of the tasks and activities which they are governing … they struggled to explain how boards should monitor student achievement and how principal's appraisal should be conducted. Without direct experience of these activities, they are forced to rely on conceptions of good practice grounded in procedural rules rather than in their own experience of the activities. (Robinson et al., 2005, p. 19)

Third, conceptions of good governance were concerned with quality of relationships and communication. The report suggested that governance was an interpersonal activity with staff appreciation and minimisation of conflict underpinning decision making and action and "such cordiality may come at the price of mutual accountability, challenge and capacity building" (Robinson et al., 2005, p. 19).

In terms of board accountability, Robinson et al. (2005) claim that lay governance appears neither educational nor democratically beneficial. Furthermore, there appears to be little effect on improving teaching, learning and achievement. The absence of educational discourse in governance was a noted area of concern. While trustees acknowledged that they represented local community interests, such representation failed to be clearly articulated or discussed in relation to governance. Possible explications for this were trustees' limited educational knowledge, difficulty in appreciating or serving local community needs and absence of legislative information to help them understand the democratic nature of their roles and responsibilities. Swamped with legislative task requirements, there appeared to be neither time nor inclination for trustees to pursue educational purpose or engage in dialogue pertaining to improving learning or teaching and the tensions this created had detrimental implications for capacity building for improvement. In other words, overtly managerialist tendencies and limited knowledge of school systems limited trustees' involvement in capacity building practices with a view to promoting school improvement. *Tomorrow's Schools* policies have had an impact on how schools are run. The scope for building capacity is very much dependent on stakeholders with knowledge of how best to craft practice (within government policy guidelines) to initiate and sustain improvement.

The Varied Nature of Low Socio economic Contexts

Adding to the milieu of tensions affecting stakeholders' ability to build capacity are challenges a multi-cultural, low socio-economic location presents. In today's society, schools are increasingly multicultural (Alton Lee, 2003; ERO, 2000; MOE, 2004) required to respond to immediate needs of diverse student/community populations. However, as ERO (2000) explains, respective legislative guidelines appear nebulous with schools experiencing difficulty interpreting goals and ascertaining if equity targets are being met in practice. Problems associated with multiculturalism extend beyond that of culture (ERO, 2000). Multicultural schools, generally located in poor socio-economic areas, may experience limited parental involvement and, in some cases, poor governance and management and weak or failed teaching provisions (ERO, 1996, 2006b). Robinson et al. (2005), reporting on governance issues in low decile schools, question the ability of boards to contribute to capacity building for improvement based on their limited understanding of role requirements and 'good' governance, lack of first-hand experience of tasks and activities over which they are governing and conceptions of 'good' governance related to communicating appreciation and minimisation of conflict rather than mutual accountability, challenge and capacity building talk.

Hawk and Hill (1997), in their AIMHI study, identified selected policies, differing home-school expectations and "low incomes, high unemployment or high over-employment, large families, dysfunctional families, poor housing, overcrowding, poor health, lack of private space and lack of furnishings and household equipment" (p. 4) as generating learning, health, social, economic and welfare needs. Hawk and Hill conclude that low socio-economic factors have implications on schools and their capacity to improve student learning outcomes. The varied nature of schools means that a one size fits all approach to building capacity and demarcating what this means for improvement will not work. What is needed is an understanding of context and school stakeholders' drive, commitment and capabilities to initiate practices that build capacity for improvement.

THEORETICAL MODEL OF CAPACITY BUILDING FOR SCHOOL IMPROVEMENT

Capacity building for school improvement is difficult to define. The definitions provided earlier do not fully explain the concept in context. Context in itself is a multi-dimensional concept that requires deconstruction. Schools are embedded in external (macro) and internal (micro) contexts within which capacity building for improvement eventuates. Both external and internal determinants of context influence how the construct is conceived. For example, values, beliefs and norms of an external context, coupled with those of an internal context influence the development of a particular mindset and specific improvement outcomes. These determinants influence the making and taking of decisions to build capacity responsive of situated need. Decision making in a landscape filled with competing accountability, compliance and reform agendas requires commitment to doing what is right for the school and its stakeholders within legislative guidelines.

Capacity building for school improvement is a time and context dependent construct. Its conceptualisation is unique to setting. Findings from this case study suggest that the ability to respond to the varied tensions of context (internal and external) in ways that meet individual, collective and systemic need not only sustains equilibrium but, also, initiates the drive to build capacity for improvement. The focus is always on change and the management of change. Capacity building is a crafted activity undertaken by school stakeholders in response to context and driven by a desire for improvement.

The capacity building for school improvement model (see Figure 9.1) places school vision at the core of all activity. Vision is considered an attribute along with stakeholders as change agents, school culture and professional development to determine the nature of practice. All four attributes account for three key capacity building practices: knowledge production and utilisation, a 'switching on' mentality; and division of labour: roles and responsibilities. The interplay of attributes and practices produces four interconnected themes that underscore the capacity building for improvement model. These include: situated activity; connectedness; governance, leadership and management; and outcomes. Capacity building for improvement is a situated activity, embedded in context. It requires connectedness explained as meaningful relationships in support of activities that 'promote student learning'. Stakeholders govern, lead and manage their schools. Their attributes, skills, roles and responsibilities are crucial in informing practice. Outcomes are a response to the situated needs of context. Reflection on outcomes, fed back into practice, promote ongoing cycles of capacity building for school improvement. Figure 9.1 captures the complexity of the construct and the interconnection among its components within the parameters of an external/internal interface.

CONCLUSION

This chapter set the scene within which capacity building for school improvement is embedded. It provides a glimpse of an external macro level context riddled with complexities and tensions that impact on the work of school leaders and educators in building capacity for improvement. The model portrayed in this chapter is deconstructed in the chapters that follow starting with attributes and progressing to practices. Chapter 2 examines the importance of vision in capacity building. Chapters 3, 4 and 5 explore the other attributes of stakeholders as change agents, school culture and professional development and the contributions each make to capacity building for school improvement. Chapters 6, 7 and 8 capture the nature of practice namely: knowledge production and utilisation; 'switching on' mentality; and division of labour: roles and responsibilities. Theorising about capacity building for school improvement occurs in Chapter 9.

NOTES

[vi] The National Education Guidelines were established in 1990 and were revised in 1993 and again in 1996. They are given effect by sections 60A and 61 of the Education Act 1989: *Every charter and proposed charter shall be deemed to contain the aim of achieving, meeting, and following (as the case may be) the National Education Guidelines* (section 61 (2)). The National Education Guidelines have three components: National Education Goals (NEGs), National Curriculum Statements and the National Administration Guidelines (NAGs).

[vii] The education review Office (ERO), Career Services (ECD), New Zealand Qualifications Authority (NZQA), New Zealand Council for Educational Research (NZCER), Learning Media, Group Special Education (GSE), Tertiary Education Commission (TEC) and the Teachers Council.

[viii] Best evidence syntheses cover, for example:
- Quality Teaching for Diverse Students in Schooling: Best Evidence Synthesis (Alton-Lee, 2003)
- Quality Teaching: Early Foundations (Farquhar, 2003)
- Professional Development in Early Childhood Settings (Mitchell & Cubey, 2003)
- The Complexity of Community and Family Influences on Children's Achievement in New Zealand: Best Evidence Synthesis (Biddulph, Biddulph & Biddulph, 2003).

[viii] Examples include: Review of Future-focused Research on Teaching and Learning (Codd, Brown, Clark, McPherson, O'Neill, O'Neill, Waitere-Ang, & Zepke, 2005); The Impact of Family and Community Resources on Student Outcomes: An assessment of the International Literature with Implications for New Zealand (Nechyba, McEwan, & Older-Aguilar, 2005); and Literature Review on the Effective Engagement of Pasifika Parents & Communities in Education (Gorinski & Fraser, 2006).

[ix] The role of ERO is "The purpose of ERO reviews is to contribute to improved student achievement. When ERO reviews schools it has a key interest in information that the school has about student achievement and also looks at the way in which school programmes and processes contribute to this achievement" (ERO, 2006a, p. 1).

SCHOOL ATTRIBUTE

Vision

Findings from the study reveal that there are four key attributes that contribute to capacity building for improvement. These are: vision; stakeholders as change agents; school culture; and professional development. Chapters 2, 3, 4 and 5 examine each through the lens of external (macro) and internal (micro) contextual determinants that influence their construction and contribution to the capacity building process. The synergistic integration of all attributes leads to the development of capacity building practices, namely: knowledge production and utilisation; 'switching on' mentality; and division of labour: roles and responsibilities. In Chapter 2, the focus is on vision and its contribution to capacity building for school improvement.

THE IMPORTANCE OF VISION

Establishing vision is something all educators agree is essential if change is likely to have any real chance of success (Barth, 1990). Weller, Hartley and Brown (1994) define vision as an all encompassing driving force of organisations to express their unique purpose and philosophy. According to Barth (1990), visions are inspirational. They depict, "an overall conception of what the educator wants the organisation to stand for: what its primary mission is; what its basic core values are; a sense of how all the parts fit together; and above all, how the vision maker fits into the grand plan" (p. 148). Shared vision or the glue that binds the school together constitutes a moving force or synergy to effect change (ibid.). West et al. (2000), in *Moving Schools Project,* note that "The evolution of vision becomes a stage which makes meaning of the improvement journey as it evolves" (p. 39). Fullan (1993) notes that vision emerges from more than it precedes action and shared vision resulting from the dynamic interaction of organisational members and leaders is vital for improvement. All this takes time and will not succeed unless the vision building process is somewhat open-ended and pursued authentically while avoiding premature formalisation.

The findings from this study reveal that vision forms the heart of all capacity building for school improvement activity. Three reasons account for this. First, vision conceptualisation, transmission and evolution forms an ongoing act of 'deliberate choice' by stakeholders in response to macro and micro cultural values and contextual need. In this school, the vision is articulated as 'striving to be the best in promoting student learning'. It is supported by four tenets of student centred learning, improvement mindset, empowerment and community. Adherence to the four tenets ensures vision provides a platform for meeting school stakeholders' need in building capacity for school improvement. Second, vision espousal and enactment serves as a cornerstone for managing tensions of external and internal contexts. Adherence to the tenets informs decisions taken to minimise limitations and maximise opportunities to benefit the school and its stakeholders. Third, vision construction is time and context dependent. Although the vision in its current form has historical antecedents and current applicability, it also contains a futuristic outlook. The power of this school's vision stems from its situated perspective and continuous evolution to accommodate need in response to: Whose vision is being promoted? How is vision linked to capacity building for improvement? And, what processes lead to its generation and evolution? Attempts to answer these questions cement attention on purpose – striving to be the best in promoting student learning.

EXTERNAL AND INTERNAL INFLUENCES ON VISION

The vision of an organisation is a social construct created within spheres of external (macro) and internal (micro) influences. External influences on a school's vision in New Zealand can be traced to the Ministry of Education, outside agencies and the local community. The Ministry of Education's influence occurs through *The National Education Guidelines* set within current law[x] and Acts of Parliament. In the case study school, strategic plans are linked to the vision and indicate compliance with government legislative mandates. The vision is underpinned by commonly held values espoused by the Ministry of Education in *The New Zealand Curriculum Framework* (1993) namely: honesty, reliability, respect for others, respect for the law, tolerance, fairness, caring or compassion, non-sexism and non-racism. The vision is also linked to staff and community held values and beliefs such as collaboration in ways of working together to achieve goals, commitment in making this school the best, learning inclusive of all stakeholders and organisation, planning and structure that make this school a 'safe place'. Matters of staying abreast of curriculum and pedagogical changes, having an approachable school, parent education, building community and celebrating difference influence behaviour patterns atypical to this site.

Successive Ministry of Education policies influence the school's vision. For example, the parent mentoring initiative with its aim to strengthen partnerships between parents and schools is fully supported by school stakeholders. The school recognises and delivers on its statutory and administrative obligations covering curriculum delivery, property, personnel, financial and health and safety requirements. Responding to such requirements can create tensions in practice as the vision, meant to be inspirational, has an added attachment of meeting regulatory mandates. The school manages such tensions by adhering to the principle of doing what's best for all stakeholders. Compliance measures are addressed but so too are matters of educational importance. In response to external/internal influences, the vision:

– Focuses attention on practices that promote student centred learning;

- Initiates an improvement mindset;
- Encourages a sense of empowerment; and
- Strengthens community involvement to benefit the school.

The extent and nature of outside agency influences on vision is related to programmes that have particular appeal and/or that result from courses, conferences and business enterprises. Although these stand unrelated (directly) to *The National Education Guidelines* and Acts of Parliament, the influences from such sources permeate school boundaries to influence direction. The school's buy-in to the 'You Can Do It'[xi] programme, for example, has had a huge influence on the vision so much so that staff and parents claim that it underpins everything that happens here.

Internal influences on vision occur in response to meeting stakeholder and school needs as identified through systemic reviews and practices. Reviews represent opportunities to reflect and make future plans (see Figure 5.1). They tend to be forecasting tools *with data looked at and discussed in terms of positives and negatives and where we need to pick up and where our future focus needs to be.* Daily practices exert influence in as much the same way as reviews. They involve all stakeholders *leading by example.* Addressing school and stakeholder needs through monitoring of practice and reviews generates *real commitment to making a difference* and ensuring that the vision has a strong foothold in reality and its implementation is the result of collaboration and collective ownership.

A SOCIALLY CONSTRUCTED VISION

The vision, articulated as 'striving to be the best in promoting student learning' is an inspirational ideal that unites staff, parents, students, outside agencies, Ministry officials and businesses in supporting the school. Barth (1990) claims vision binds people to a common cause. This appears to be the case in this school. The school's vision as a confluence of macro and micro values underpins what stakeholders call 'work' in alignment to the four tenets of student centred learning, improvement mindset, empowerment and community. The mission statement, *I can do it, you can do it and together we can achieve our goals* is an empowering mantra that enhances a 'work hard' for improvement ethic. The vision is portrayed as a living document; a purveyor of hope in a context where tensions of funding, accountability and compliance, low socio-economic factors and multi-ethnic considerations can limit efforts to build capacity for improvement.

The school's vision is grounded in a reality base and its evolution considered a continuous process. Stakeholders' input in vision conceptualisation, transmission and evolution makes them agents of change. Their transformative agency is not without tensions, however, as decisions concerning school direction and goal setting are debated from particular group values and beliefs. Contestation of values and beliefs challenge the existing status quo of 'how things are done around here' (Deal & Kennedy, 1982, 1983). Such challenges raise doubt defined by Schechter (2004) as an honourable moral objective facilitating growth and dialogue around purpose. Debates that raise doubt lead to vision evolution and encourage what Annan et al. (2003) regard as 'learning talk'.

In this school site, opportunities for learning talk encourage collaborative interchange, reflection, 'openness to new ideas' and value debates. They occur at all levels (school professional development meetings, team and curriculum meetings and home-school partnership events) to create dialogue around purpose - promoting student learning through effective practice. Collective examination of philosophies, ideologies, values and beliefs maintain a grounded reality base from which to make and take authentic decisions for the good of the stakeholders in this school. School improvement is gauged against external and internal benchmarks documented in the strategic plans. Written documentation inspires purpose driven action. The energy and drive to sustain improvement over time is hard work given challenges of setting. However, the school's vision fuels the much needed energy to maximise efforts to build capacity for improvement according to 'fit'. The vision is not only a force for change but, also, reinforces the four tenets of student centred learning, improvement mindset, empowerment and community. As a socially constructed tool, it provides a 'blueprint' or 'map' for action.

CENTRAL TENNETS

External and internal influences on the vision generate the four tenets of student centred learning, improvement mindset, empowerment and community. These are endorsed by school stakeholders who claim that *if you know what the vision is and agree with it then that is your purpose and everyone will work together to achieve the same goal.* In the sections that follow, each tenet is explained from various stakeholders' perspectives.

Student Centred Learning

Student centred learning represents a call for action. The principal comments, *it is the whole reason for our being here.* The deputy principal claims, *if you think about any of us that is why we are here ... doing the best thing for the children ... in the classroom, in curriculum areas, in the environment of the school.* Teaching staff comments endorse senior management claims as, for example, *raising expectations is about giving children something to aspire to ... it's about how much we care about the children so let's give them the best.* Parents maintain, *this school teaches a child specifically to raise their level; You know it's about getting the children to achieve just not on an academic level but grow within themselves and become good people at the end of the day; educated the right way;* and *with other races because it is a very multi-cultural school.*

A focus on student centred learning means: improvement in class environments, *to show what the children have done;* holistic attendance to student need (academic, physical, artistic, behaviour, social and emotional); and meeting ethnic diversity through systems, processes and structural support, *you know we have got such a diverse multi-cultural population here that I would hope that valuing and supporting each other and the cultures would be part of it too.* Practical support in meeting cultural needs means running cultural programmes, adjusting practice in ways that are culturally appropriate and employing auxiliary staff to support students and their families.

Student centred learning means inclusion of families in the learning process. Parents' knowledge capacities are enhanced by engagement in home-school partnership programmes and parent chat sessions. The school advocates an open door policy where parents are welcomed and encouraged to participate in all school activities. Building parents' educational knowledge creates an inclusive learning environment which serves the best interest of students and ultimately advances the 'striving to be the best in promoting student learning' vision ideal.

Improvement Mindset

School stakeholders claim an improvement mindset is omnipresent and means, *working with what you have got but continually trying to make things better.* An improvement mindset is defined as:

> *We are trying to improve children's learning. Trying to make it a positive place where everyone is growing, staff, the children and that the teachers are professional. I wouldn't call it a stagnant school as it is making every effort to improve in different ways: the children's learning, the room environments, the school environment and the school's image in the wider community.*

An improvement mindset has many dimensions. In terms of structure, the comments made were: *the furniture has been painted, the handrail has been done. I think it impacts on the kids because they are in a bright attractive environment.* Improving the image of the school involves all stakeholders getting involved and working together *showing care, ownership, understanding and working together for a common goal which is for the betterment of the school.* Care, ownership, understanding and working together achieve vision goals related to improvement. An improvement mindset related to raising academic and behaviour expectations means, *making sure that it has quality programmes operating – not just anything.* Raising staff expectations means taking on board new ideas and strategies that *flow into the classrooms with children knowing what's expected.*

Comments from staff indicate that an improvement mindset *needs to be felt by the people.* Feeling the need for change means *people know that things need to get better* and engaging in purpose-driven action. For staff, an improvement mindset means increased professionalism. Professionalism linked to improvement involves: Individualised learning: *teachers set their own goals and those that trickle down to the children. Goal setting is a big thing and it's really up to us*;

Collective learning: *There's a lot more ownership now of where we are going to meet the needs ... a team thing and we can see the purpose to it*; and *because everyone is there at that same meeting we are all getting the same message. It means we all know what we are meant to be doing and we know what we are expected to do*;

25

Monitored practice: *upskilling the staff and then the monitoring that happens within the classrooms as well*; and *actually following things through and looking at work so that we're monitoring the children and we know what's happening*;

Focused attention on quality: *actually making sure that we are doing justice to each thing that is happening and making sure we are not just giving lip-service*;

Working towards a common goal: *it all becomes part of your daily plan*; and

Future planning and goal achievement: *We had all these lovely ideas of making changes and doing different things in the school. And now if you look, we are achieving them.*

Empowerment

Empowerment is linked to principles that underpin the 'You Can Do It' programme. Staff note this equates to *kids out there who are succeeding and are leaders and that our school is at the cutting edge offering a range of top quality programmes*. The 'You Can Do It' programme has increased the positive ethos in the school. For students this means behavioural and attitudinal changes related to learning: *You hear different kids encouraging each other like in athletics or different things. You hear different comments from teachers that different kids have made encouraging comments in different ways.* For parents it means having a go and getting involved. The 'You Can Do It' programme has had an empowering effect on staff. The following, very personal quote by a staff member, highlights this:

I'm meant to be telling the children about being confident and all the rest ... but sometimes I don't feel confident and so how can I be out there telling them and trying to develop their confidence thinking my own is lacking. I have had to change my attitude. Not only do I have to start thinking more confidently but also acting a bit more confidently.

Empowerment is played out in shared leadership. To illustrate, sustainability of the 'You Can Do It' programme is officially the special education coordinator's responsibility who notes, y*ou can say at the moment that I am the leader of it.* However, because the programme underscores practice and is accepted philosophy, the responsibility is also that belonging to everyone. Empowerment extends to staff sharing leadership responsibilities in educational matters. As observed in meetings, teachers accept lead roles for knowledge acquisition, distribution, implementation and change of practice.

Empowerment involves parents as partners in various school activities. A reciprocal relationship exists where staff and parents support each other in governance, decision-making, fund raising and networking roles. The school supports parent involvement through such means as employing bi-lingual support workers to help bridge the home-school divide for families so as to optimise student learning. At home-school partnership evenings, teachers and parents provide community members with information about curriculum developments. Staff-led parent chat sessions provide opportunities to build community knowledge on education, health and positive parenting. Empowerment of parents is seen to increase home-school partnerships. Parent volunteers help in managing school resources, assist in class, participate in cultural group activities and provide support in activities such as sports and school trips.

Empowerment is captured by the shared language of school stakeholders. Stakeholders use 'we' and phrases such as 'harnessed together' to denote 'community' and 'togetherness'. Community builds trust and in an atmosphere of trust, asking questions, seeking clarification and taking collective action flourish. There is an expectation that everyone contributes in decision-making and shares in task accomplishment: *I think with our team it is expected that everybody takes a part in meetings; the whole team is taking on board more the sharing of responsibility.* The ability to raise doubt, voice opinion and seek clarification increases empowerment in one's ability to initiate change for purpose.

Community

A central tenet of this school's vision is building community. Community has numerous defining elements. According to the deputy principal, community is an all inclusive term, *not just for the kids but for the home and the school and we work together as a community. We have fun.* For parents, community is, *trying to get the parents involved. You know it's not just up to the teachers and the principal and deputy.* The concept of community has roots in the past but appears to be an evolving construct. The principal notes that *in this community there has always been a big heart. I noticed when I came to this school how friendly the children were and also the staff and parents. That was a culture that had been in the school but there wasn't a working culture. They were friendly but they didn't seem to be working.*

Community now means pulling in the same direction and working collaboratively: *a team thing and we can see what we are doing things for and the purpose to it and we are helping each other and appreciating each other.* A collaborative work culture is enhanced by school systems, processes and structures. For example, in the initial phase of school improvement, the principal created a central resource storage area *so there wasn't any of this is mine and yours.* Comments from staff endorse such action as enhancing the professionalism of a school community.

Community means showing respect for all cultures by valuing diversity. As acknowledged by the principal, *you know we have got such a diverse multi-cultural population here that I would hope that we all value and support each other and appreciating other cultures would be part of it too. It is a multi-cultural school and it shows respect for everyone.*

Stakeholders associate community with feeling safe and this represents:
- Ability to express voice;
- Participation in collaborative decision making;
- Engagement in shared dialogue desirous of learning; and
- Acceptance of others' viewpoints.

Community means inclusion of parents in the decision making process. As highlighted in construction of consecutive strategic plans, parents' aspirations and views are given serious consideration. Goal setting works towards meeting staff, students' and parents' requirements. There is an expectation that this school, given its low socio-economic location and ethnic diversity, assists in the building of parents' knowledge capacity. This viewpoint is justified on the basis that informed parents contribute as partners in education generating capacity for improvement.

VISION CONSTRUCTION: CONCEPTUALISATION, TRANSMISSION AND EVOLUTION

Vision construction involves conceptualisation, transmission and evolution. Successive strategic plans, linked to vision, record goals and steps taken towards goal achievement based on systemic reviews and parents/staff collaboration on school direction.

Vision Conceptualisation

Stakeholders' claim the vision is grounded in what is considered important. The process symbolises recognition and acting on stakeholder voice: *We have talked about it. It's up on the wall in the staff room.* Vision construction has an evidential base, initiated, in the beginning, by the principal who *ran surveys and interviews just to find out what people said.* Staff feel they are listened to and their opinions valued: *The things we were talking about were the issues and we have a say in things and that's why the school is open to ideas.*

Strategic plans, traceable to the school's vision, involve all school stakeholders in their conceptualisation. This ensures 'fit' with school stakeholders' views and contextual needs. Staff and parents are vision creators, implementers and guardians. Their collective input builds on past experiences to eventuate change that is grounded in current practice with future goals in mind.

Vision conceptualisation and steps taken towards achievement of goals necessitates continuous systemic and academic reviews, an analysis of which indicates:
– Teamness, a sharing of views with others to promote agreed goals for future action;
– Accountability of goal achievement – progress made is 'ticked off' and next steps added;
– Room for individual, collective and systemic growth;
– Transparency of past and current achievements combined with future goals; and
– Compliance to Ministry of Education demands that renders this school a 'safe place'.

Vision Transmission

The vision is transmitted in a variety of ways. Articulation by staff is one source of transmission. For example, scheduled times for the teaching of 'You Can Do It', altered teaching strategies in response to the needs of students, collective engagement in activities and community involvement in home-school partnerships indicate a buy-in to the four tenets. Newsletters promote the vision out in the community. Establishment of the parents' room enforces the message that parents are welcome in the school and that this is a community school with an open door policy. Cultural artefacts on display espouse vision messages. For example, 'You Can Do It' signs and posters are visually displayed around the school. A section of wall space in all classes is devoted to promoting 'You Can Do It' ideals. Certificates and end of the year cups and trophies achieve similar purpose of validating the vision and its tenets.

Students articulate vision messages. On the topic of 'You Can Do It', comments received by staff, from students, denote assimilation and enactment of programme ideals. Parent involvement in school life and active participation in home-school partnership and parent chat programmes help transmit the vision. The claim is: *If other parents see that these parents can do it then they think that we can do it too; like people will see the school as a safe place of learning.*

School systems, processes and structures enhance vertical and horizontal transmission of the vision. For example, at whole staff, team and parents meetings, vision ideals are explicitly and implicitly endorsed. The strategic plans and reviews engineer collaborative reflection and renewal of vision that maintains its currency. Such documents serve as monitoring devices: *if you look at all those things in the strategic plans, we are achieving them.*

Vision Evolution

Vision evolution is a result of continuous reflective practice. Reflection on practice reduces diversion away from goal achievement. Reflective practice focuses on promoting student learning by attending to planning, teaching, learning and evaluation. The message continually enforced is, 'striving to be the best in promoting student learning'. Capacity building is enhanced because, *the vision focuses you and you have it in your head and sometimes you go on little tangents or lots of little tangents so you need to refocus and re-look at where you are heading.*

Reflection on practice means concerted attention to all four tenets. It means constantly being aware of what the vision is and whether the pathway to its achievement is undertaken authentically. Examples of reflection on practice abound in this setting. The levelling or moderation of student writing samples provides an example of collective reflective practice described as:

> *I think it is about talking and discussing and trying things out. Seeing what works. Sometimes you think it is going to work but actually trying it out and then going back and doing some reviews and finding out where we are at and*

29

what are we going to do to improve ... And assisting everybody to get to where we want to get to and then looking back further and thinking we got there or even if we didn't get there thinking back, reflecting individually and with the whole school.

Monitored practice offers an approach to vision renewal. The strategic plans and self and system reviews provide transparent ways to report on progress and achievement to staff, parents, board of trustees, Ministry of Education officials and ERO. Reporting on progress reinforces connection to vision as this comment suggests, *As soon as we started I did feel "Wow there is a lot to do" and I felt tired. But as we all pulled together we have got things changed as a team. When I look at that chart now I think, "Wow we have achieved such a lot". I feel proud of that.*

CLOSING THE VISION/REALITY GAP

'Striving to be the best in promoting student learning' is an inspirational ideal, articulated, enacted and recorded in strategic plans. However, situational factors connected with funding shortages, lack of time, low socio-economic location factors and, to an extent, parent reluctance to get involved, limit achievement of vision goals. They create a vision/reality gap.

School stakeholders stated that vision implementation and school improvement were impeded by funding shortages. Examples provided related to ICT, in particular lack of equipment to capitalise on newly acquired teaching skills. Although budget restrictions and economic imperatives are an accepted reality, this school's culture of commitment and entrepreneurialism appears to absorb negative reactions associated with fiscal restrictions. Cultural norms of self-governance and self-management are promoted in minimising limitations and maximising opportunities to counteract the effects of funding shortfalls. The atmosphere that prevails is one of utilising what is available in 'striving to be the best in promoting student learning'.

School participants mentioned time limitations, fitting things in and consolidation of new learning as limiting factors. Timetabling the teaching of 'You Can Do It' and business of classroom life were cited as examples of lack of time to achieve vision goals. Senior managers display an awareness of time limitations and measures taken to counteract this include: designing flexible professional development agendas (individualised learning), encouraging staff ownership in decision-making, collective participation in task accomplishment and scaffolded assistance (teacher release, professional development and/or mentoring/coaching assistance) in goal achievement. In this setting, continuous professional development offers opportunities for learning and support.

Factors associated with the school's socio-economic context limits vision realisation. Staff comment that energy spent on managing student behaviour, dealing with student health needs, lack of pre-school education, deprived housing conditions and needs of parents makes this school challenging: *children here are from very different families that won't all fit into this one idea of maybe a white middle class Christian one – one dad, one mum, another brother/sister family*; and *'You Can Do It' programme is good for them it but becomes a little lost as soon as they walk out the gate. They have to turn it off as it is often the opposite at home. Sometimes we fight a losing battle.*

The school attempts to address community needs through provision of programmes that benefit and build parent capacity. School practices ensure staff get support in undertaking their teaching duties. Support staff are employed to specifically bridge the home-school gap. All endeavours are attempts to address challenges of location from a community, systemic perspective. Limited parental involvement, a perceived barrier to vision realisation, was mentioned by parent representatives. The school's attempt to increase this is acknowledged as:

Like most schools our parent involvement may not be as strong as other schools but it is being developed with ideas like morning jump jams and inviting parents along to parent chat meetings. The school is open to parents but with some parents it is about breaking the barriers they themselves may have about their own school life.

VISION: CAPACITY BUILDING LINKS

The focus of this book is on capacity building for school improvement. Having a vision informing practice builds capacity because it is shared, aligned with legislative requirements and geared to purpose; that is, meeting staff, students' and parents' needs and aspirations. With collective purpose comes passion for goal achievement. School participants describe the vision as contagious, *people catch on*. The vision creates a groundswell of support that ignites commitment to the 'striving to be the best in promoting student learning' vision ideal.

Purpose, accompanied by shared language, promotes common messages and shared meanings. People in this school talk about the vision, use the same language in conversations and believe in the same ideals: *It's not about having messages but ensuring that everyone is getting that same message. Everyone is working towards those goals.* From a position of common messages and shared meaning, coherence ensues. Coherence is witnessed in ways of working together, agreeing to expectations of practice consistency and facilitating a unified approach to building capacity for school improvement.

Working towards vision involves translating the vision ideal into a workable blueprint as recorded in subsequent strategic plans. Strategic plans draw on collective stakeholder input towards setting goals and designing action steps towards their achievement. A strong focus on expectations and detailing what this means in practice makes improvement easier to manage. It promotes efficiency and effectiveness in working towards vision; an attribute of capacity building.

Practices that support vision implementation also promote its buy-in. For example, strategic plans not only record future school directions but are accountability tools that attest to progress made. They generate professional dialogue around the tenets of student centred learning, an improvement mindset, empowerment and community. Such engagement affirms and increases stakeholder commitment to overall vision direction in building capacity for improvement.

Stakeholders' role in vision conceptualisation, transmission and evolution engenders collective activity around doing the best for this school. In vision transmission and evolution, school stakeholders, *regularly re-look at the vision* leading to its modification in line with changing internal and external conditions: *Well whenever we plan we think about how appropriate it is for other cultures.* Processes of evolution keep the vision alive and current. A 'readiness' or 'preparedness' for change ensue as school systems, processes, and structures are primed to meet new demands; crucial in building capacity for improvement.

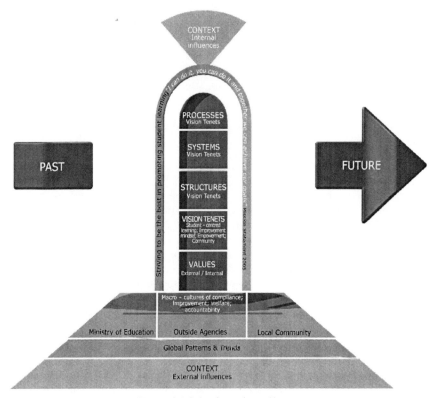

Figure 2.1 School Attribute: Vision

CONCLUSION

This school's vision is inspirational in that its key message espouses the 'striving to be the best in promoting student learning' ideal. The vision is recorded in successive strategic plans. As such it offers a blueprint or map for practice. Figure 2.1 highlights the influences on vision. It captures diagrammatically the vision ideal with its empowering mission statement *I can do it, you can do it and together we can achieve our goals.* Underpinning tenets of student centred learning, improvement mindset, empowerment and community are placed at the centre depicting connection to school systems, processes and structures. The vision unifies and grounds stakeholders to what is important – promoting student learning. As a combined package inclusive of conceptualisation, transmission and evolution processes, the vision serves to guide the building of capacity for school improvement that is situated, embedded in practice and reflective of macro and micro influences.

NOTES

[x] The Education Act (1989), Treaty of Waitangi (1840), Crimes Act (1961), Public Finance Act (1989), Crown Entities Act (2005) to name but a few.

[xi] You Can Do It Education was founded in Australia in 1991. The founder is Dr. Michael Bernard. It relates to assisting children to realise their potential and to achieve to the best of their ability in school work and other areas of endeavour. It is based on four foundations: confidence, persistence, getting along, and organisation. It extends to student development, parent education and school professional development.

SCHOOL ATTRIBUTES

Stakeholders as Change Agents

Leadership in today's complex environment requires the efforts of many rather than a few to create change (Harris & Lambert, 2003; Fullan, 2002). Contemporary models of leadership for school improvement indicate movement away from leader-centrism and heroism towards shared, collective, collaborative and collegial practices with norms of mutual influence and community (Evans-Andris, 2010; Gronn, 2002). Smylie, Conley and Marks (2002) note that leadership performed across roles from both formal and informal positions of authority is more productive in enhancing communication, problem solving, developing innovative instructional practice and capacity building. In contemporary work settings, the focus on distributed practice as opposed to formal hierarchical authority highlights less control and more reliance on the contributions of others to work productively within a division of labour paradigm; a contrast to traditional hierarchical practices (Harris, 2004). An emphasis on this way of working heightens the necessity for trust, collaboration, professional learning and reciprocal accountability when working together (Copland, 2003). The role stakeholders' play in building capacity for improvement is grounded in such interactions. Smylie, Wendt and Fendt (2003) note that in schools displaying distributed practice, tasks such as vision sustainment, promotion of coherence, building knowledge and skills and monitoring programme implementation are performed in coordinated ways by multiple actors. Coming from a position of distributed practice and division of labour, this chapter considers the work of stakeholders as change agents and the impact this has on capacity building for improvement.

For this study, stakeholders involved included the principal, deputy and assistant principals, teachers, auxiliary staff and parents. As core players in activities that build capacity for improvement they uphold the view that managing challenges of site for improvement proves effective when distributed across groups. In order to discuss how stakeholders as change agents form an attribute of capacity building for improvement, delineation of contextual challenges and stakeholder activity by way of mitigation to establish equilibrium and sustain improvement is important. The discussion posited in this chapter starts by recapping contextual challenges and discussing stakeholder responses in minimising challenges and maximising opportunities to build capacity. The concept of stakeholders as change agents is discussed from the view point of actions taken and contributions made to capacity building for improvement in relation to:
– Visionary leadership;

- Systemic development;
- Educational leadership; and
- Network building.

CHALLENGES OF CONTEXT AND MITIGATING RESPONSES

Challenges of context are complex, multi-faceted and reflective of an educational landscape driven by market driven ideologies. The integrated effects of a low decile location, negative school perception, interschool competition and fluctuating roll growth adversely affect a school's ability to build capacity and improve. They affect community perceptions and actions as this comment captures:

> *I live 500 metres from the school and a lot of people take their kids off to other schools ... it is very much perceived as a low decile school and there's a perception out there that you don't (if you're middle class) take them off and send them to a decile two school; and once that reputation starts everyone knows about it and it's just hard to stop. I think schools should have a fair and reasonable zone. Those who are in the zone[xii] should go to that school.*

Such comments typify problems of perception this school faces that are difficult to address and shift. A perception of this school as multicultural generates a hesitancy to enrol students here. This, coupled with inter-school competition for students, raises possibilities of roll decline contributing to funding reduction. The talk that circulates among staff and parents confirm an awareness of pressures attached to sustaining roll growth for improvement. The ramifications of a falling roll means funding reduction with adverse budgeting and management repercussions threatening financial capacity to initiate and sustain improvement. While a prevailing feeling of vulnerability exists, an accompanying sense of strength is gained by tapping into collective capabilities of school stakeholders to counteract problems of negative school perception and the detrimental consequences of this on the school.

School stakeholders respond by actively promoting this school as 'school of choice' in the neighbourhood. This occurs through word of mouth promotional acts and the advantageous use of the local media to raise the image of this school as progressive and improving. The effort taken to bring about change of perception is time consuming and slow despite intensive efforts on the part of stakeholders to make a difference. However the, *I can do it, you can do it and together we can achieve our goals* mission statement is a force that sustains stakeholders' quest to achieve change.

Low decile challenges of location have additional implications for school personnel in terms of meeting students' and the parents' diverse needs. Concerns raised by staff relate to an inability to communicate with *parents that don't have English as a first language; doing additional work outside the classroom to build parents' knowledge base;* and *creating a community feel.* In a school with many different cultures, language barriers among community groups cause problems of establishing meaning and enlisting support when it comes to student learning and building community spirit. Such challenges of location demand action aimed at *including the community and making parents aware of what's happening and what's required and what they need to do to help kids.* Action taken by school staff involves ensuring that teaching and learning pedagogies are directed at meeting students' needs in a planned, systematic manner. Parents are brought on board through home-school partnership activities focused on increasing their involvement and raising collective community awareness on matters of education.

Complexities of context demand action not only in the area of catering for diverse students' and parents' needs but, also, staying abreast of government initiatives in curriculum and policy. Meeting external change demands necessitates *getting the balance right and finding the balance between lots of new learning and work load.* Time spent debating how change demands are to be implemented, preparing for implementation, implementation and follow up checks to ensure implementation does happen addresses macro and micro calls for change. However, such processes take time and energy to enact and appear particularly demanding on the principal and deputy principal who 'walk' staff and board members through new legislative and curriculum requirements. By way of facilitating change, senior managers encourage collaborative decision-making to ensure vision-led goals are achieved together with government legislation and reform mandates.

The literature is amass with assertions that change disestablishes equilibrium and, if not managed, leads to role confusion, added responsibilities and unclear expectations. Change and the need for change are here to stay. School stakeholders faced continuously with multidimensional and complex change demands find themselves adapting to new 'ways of doing things'. In the New Zealand context, for example, complete or partial change to board membership every three years is an example of imposed legislative change necessitating stakeholder adjustment to a new regime of governance. It leads to inevitable flow-on adjustments and accommodation in practice. The new board or members have to be inducted on matters of school operations and governance roles and responsibilities. They have to be 'walked' through what is expected of them as governors of the school in dealing with compliance and legislative responsibilities. The responsibility for this falls on the principal and deputy principal.

The call for change to improve teaching and learning practice is also internally driven considered something schools do periodically to improve. Internal change can be traced to audits and reviews conducted by school stakeholders on systems, processes and structures. In this site, curriculum and systemic reviews conducted periodically produce data which is analysed and reflected on to ascertain pathways for improvement (see Figure 5.1). Management of pedagogical change to improve teaching and learning is managed and scaffolded by all stakeholders working together.

Unexpected random calls for change (sudden staff departure, for example) necessitate immediate action and the school's ability to deal with the rapidity of such change may cause duress. Here, the school's ability to cope indicates not only reliance on systems, processes and structures to buffer and absorb flow on change demands but, also, goodwill towards others in time of need. Regardless of type, all change, planned and unplanned, has repercussions: growing uncertainty, increased workload and so forth. Successful management of change not only calls for robust systems, processes and structures but, also, the ways by which people are able to handle themselves in midst of upheaval. In this respect the personal attributes of stakeholders count as significant.

PERSONAL ATTRIBUTES OF SCHOOL STAKEHOLDERS

Findings from this study reveal that school stakeholders' personal attributes matter in meeting the demands of context and change. The claims made by staff are that being positive and having a mindset on improvement is important. In this school, stakeholders' concern for social issues influences their preparedness to act as advocates for the rights of staff, students and parents. An attribute of preparedness to push the boundaries of existing practice towards improvement results from recourse to vision, a passion for the job and working in ways that benefit others.

The principal and deputy/assistant principals are awarded praise for their ability to minimise challenges of context and manage change successfully. They display positive, meaningful work relationships stemming from being *completely on the same wavelength*. They are said to have *high goodwill, emotional maturity and professional intelligence respectful of diversity. They seem to come from a place where they appreciate you. They exemplify reflective practice.* Staff and parents work in collaboration to create synergy or a motivational force that brings about change. All school stakeholders walk the talk in matters promoting student learning. They act as change agents by proactively fulfilling the parameters of their jobs and willingly engaging in a vast array of tasks and responsibilities required over and above what their positions dictate even when this generates work overload. Their change agency roles involve distributed practice enacted through visionary leadership, systemic development, educational leadership, and network building as discussed next.

CHANGE AGENCY ROLE: VISIONARY LEADERSHIP

The vision exerts a powerful force in maintaining a sense of direction that grounds people to what matters in determining and managing change aimed at 'striving to be the best in promoting student learning'. Stakeholder engagement in activities such as vision embedded strategic planning makes them advocates of the four tenets of student centred learning, improvement, empowerment and community. Open articulation of the tenets by stakeholders engenders optimism and portrayal of a collective force to manage change.

Vision-led activity as a force for change demands from school stakeholders' reflection on practice. In this school, high degrees of reflective practice results from engagement and dialogue on what it means to support the four tenets. Reflective practice makes the vision renewal process a collective

enterprise where attention is always on improvement, promoting student learning, developing a culture that values learning and building a professional learning community inclusive of all stakeholders. Vision-led activity is all inclusive. At school and board meetings, staff and parent representatives deliberate on future decisions concerning the school. At the school level, reflective practice in support of meaningful, collaborative dialogue facilitates improvement of practice through:
- Rigorous analysis of data to establish authentic points for learning and change;
- Prioritising need and formulating action plans in response to vision goals;
- Promoting improvement;
- Empowering others in goal setting, management and evaluation; and
- Celebrating achievement.

CHANGE AGENCY ROLE: SYSTEMIC DEVELOPMENT

The school is a network of complex systems, processes and structures governed by policies for curriculum, personnel, finance and property. Underpinning all policies sits the school's charter, a contract between the board of trustees and the Minister of Education to ensure that the school complies with current legislation and reports annually to the Ministry of Education on stated aims and objectives. With reference to such complex demands, each stakeholder is expected to contribute to systemic development according to their level of expertise and responsibility. The expectation is that everybody is important and, therefore, will contribute. For example, the board of trustees holds a governance role in the school. The board, in conjunction with the principal, staff and sometimes community, writes, ratifies and reviews policies. The principal manages the implementation of policies on a daily basis. Delegation of some policy implementation is awarded to staff. In this school, systems, processes and structures intended to achieve good management exist. Systems, processes and structures secure and strengthen relationships, facilitate collaborative interchange and stimulate reflection on practice. They generate opportunities for stakeholders to fulfil their delineated roles and responsibilities as well as contribute to the collective in terms of capacity building for improvement.

Sarason (1996) identifies principals as gatekeepers of change because their contribution during innovation is significant to its success. Leadership qualities of principals most readily associated with reform include: defining, managing, supervising and monitoring improvement efforts in schools (Evans-Andris, 2010). In this school, the principal, immersed in complexities of daily events, has a long range vision of systemic development. She exercises guardianship over all systems, processes and structures. Guardianship involves protecting, nurturing and maintaining systemic networks. As a systems developer, she serves as the cornerstone between students, parents and staff on the one hand and Ministry of Education and outside agencies on the other. She ensures management of change takes into consideration divergent viewpoints reflective of context.

The deputy/assistant principals' expertise and skills are seen to enhance all forms of internal systemic development. For example, over and above their

39

instructional leadership role, they are in charge of duties that are management orientated. These include, for example, change of rosters, timetables, playground duties and setting the tone for behaviour and discipline. They hold curriculum portfolios which involve them in programme construction, resource management, monitoring of work, professional development, assessment and evaluation. Alongside the principal, the deputy/assistant principals initiate and manage the collation and analysis of data. They report on analysed data to staff, parents and the board of trustees. The deputy principal supports the principal in appraising staff.

The main focus of teachers is setting up effective systems, processes and structures related to classroom activities and delivery of the curriculum. Teachers claim that high levels of systemic functioning results from:
- Time set aside for systems, processes and structural development; that is, teachers and other staff members are released to get jobs/tasks accomplished;
- Systemic coherence and practice consistency achieved through collective production and utilisation of knowledge and buy-in of all school stakeholders to vision tenets;
- Budgeted financial support and provision of resources in systemic development;
- Professional development that is continuous and aligned with systemic need;
- Accountability checks and balances to ensure systems, processes and structures are viable and robust to cope with challenges of change; and
- Communication that is transparent and *open* to ensure 'common' knowledge of systems, processes and structures.

CHANGE AGENCY ROLE: EDUCATIONAL LEADERSHIP

All school stakeholders adopt educational leadership roles. In capacities as leaders, they actively promote and manage innovation during times of change. They are instrumental in identifying, purchasing and utilising appropriate instructional materials and resources, engage in modelling and generally offer guidance to others to improve teaching and learning. As leaders they have different areas of expertise and knowledge. Their collective contributions are valued for the meaningful way they can support the building of capacity for improvement.

The principal, as lead learner and teacher, is considered, *very strong on professional development. She is always learning and she loves to learn.* As observed, a culture of learning reflects the values and beliefs of the principal *open to the academic community.* Her knowledge base of classroom practice makes her a credible educator and her pedagogical and theoretical knowledge motivates teaching staff to try out new strategies. She is able to facilitate learning environments where group interaction and dialogue are encouraged.

Similar comments are attributed to the deputy/assistant principals who are awarded praise *because they have been teachers and know the difficulties and problems that are happening in the classroom.* They have considerable knowledge of systems, processes and structures to improve practice. Their depth of understanding ensures robust systems and processes are in place for managing reviews and ensuring collected, collated and analysed data serves school and stakeholder needs. Their depth of knowledge on curriculum matters positions them as 'experts' to lead and scaffold the learning of others. These attributes and skills make them purpose-driven, action-oriented leaders facilitating knowledge flow to produce systemic cohesion that brings everyone together. In terms of change management, such actions promote change that is *realistic bite sized pieces integrated rather than just overwhelming and disorientating.*

Teaching staff communication of knowledge extends to groups they work with in teams or individually with colleagues, students, parents and outside agency representatives. Collaboration with others in promoting student learning can be evidenced at whole school, team and curriculum meetings and home-school events. Their activities contribute to a learning culture.

Parents involved with home-school partnership programmes communicate and facilitate their own educational networks. Communication of knowledge by parents involved in school life make them educational leaders outside in the community. Their ability to be effective in the transmission of knowledge occurs because they are provided with information and their ability to contribute is enhanced by the strong learning culture that prevails in this school.

CHANGE AGENCY ROLE: NETWORK BUILDING

Data from this study indicates that internal and external networks of support are established for various purposes. Whole school, professional development and year level teams and curriculum group meetings are network sites which provide opportunities for people to engage in professional dialogue. Such professional networks are vital in building a professional learning community. Community is an inclusive term incorporating not only school staff but, also, Ministry officials, outside agencies, businesses and parents. Networking promotes 'thinking outside the square' in establishing positive working relationships with those who can assist the school meet its needs. School stakeholders tap into the resources of each other to further establish networking in this school.

The school's infrastructure fosters working in teams; an organisational component fostering networking. The school is organised into junior, middle and senior teams. Teams meet once a week to attend to administration duties and engage in professional development. Observation at these meetings indicates high levels of collaborative activity aimed at task achievement. Practices of knowledge production and utilisation result from working collaboratively to develop a collective knowledge pool. Networking of this kind creates double loop learning, an essential component of capacity building as advocated by Senge (2000).

In this school, the coordination of team networking is driven by staff. They are responsible for setting budgets, maintaining resources, providing assistance when requested and reporting on progress. Membership on curriculum teams is fluid with staff opting to be members of one or more teams. Movement of staff in and among teams fosters connectedness and a sense of belonging. Knowledge development increases through being a team member. Work undertaken in this manner facilitates change management as team members are more equipped to play advisory/decision making roles. Part of team mentality is having trust in each other to act professionally and work from positions of valuing the contributions of others as individuals within a collective.

Networking, as explained, establishes professional bonds among a variety of stakeholders: parents and staff; parents, staff and students; and parents, staff, Ministry of Education, outside agencies and others. Behavioural characteristics associated with making networking successful include:

- Awareness of personal needs of colleagues, students and parents so that plans of action are formulated specific to need;
- Awareness of what is on offer in the community so quick responses are able to be made in ways that benefit the school;
- Maintaining on-going relationships with Ministry and outside agencies so that assistance, if required, can be procured; and
- Networking that continues to position the school at the cutting edge of new knowledge.

STAKEHOLDERS AS CHANGE AGENTS: CAPACITY BUILDING LINKS

Capacity building for school improvement is concerned with managing challenges and change. Changing and improving schools means coping with numerous tasks, duties and responsibilities (Evans-Andris, 2010). Such tasks include sustainment of vision, educational leadership, systemic development and networking. Change, if not managed appropriately, can disestablish equilibrium and increase uncertainty as new ways of doing things are required. Here the concept of school stakeholders as change agents becomes important. Findings from this study suggest that this school's ability to manage change necessitates all its stakeholders working as change agents. The stance promoted is best explained as appreciating what someone else has to offer and working in ways that consider individual, collective and systemic needs. As change agents, work done in teams is described as:

> *I think organisational learning is working together as a team ... everybody from the hierarchy down to the Scale A teachers. It is also helping each other to make sure we organise our planning and our resources for each lesson. If we need help we ask other people around us like teachers and parents. If we need somebody from the community to help we ask.*

Stakeholders as change agents are not prepared to adopt a reactive stance to external/internal challenges of context. Their actions and mindset suggest they scan the environment for opportunities and consider ways to make systemic adjustment and modifications in line with vision. Responses are not knee-jerk but strategically implemented through allowing time for planning, collegial discussions, teaming, and communicating which brings all on board. In managing change, challenges at the internal/external interface receive considerable attention to build capacity for school improvement.

The extent to which stakeholders as change agents are prepared to build capacity for improvement is linked to their acceptance of distributed practice. This school is marked by its division of labour ways of working. Sustainability of improvement relies on the capacity of all prepared to go the extra mile in promoting outcomes for students. Copland (2003) defines sustainability as "embedding reform work into the culture of the school" (p 393). School stakeholders in their change agency role accomplish this based on the premise that everyone has their own unique strengths and can and must contribute. Such actions sustain capacity building for the school improvement.

Figure 3.1 adds the attribute of stakeholders as change agents to Figure 2.1 where vision was positioned at the core of capacity building for school improvement. Stakeholders as change agents engage in visionary and educational leadership, system development and network building roles and responsibilities. As such they are seen to:

– Provide strong active leadership;
– Contribute in ways that inspire others;
– Contribute towards an improving school culture;
– Further the vision of the school;
– Function within role boundaries and with a preparedness to take on additional responsibilities; and
– Expand their professional capacities by participating in meaningful decision-making so as to advance capacity building for improvement.

CONCLUSION

Chapter 3 highlighted the contribution of all school stakeholders as change agents in building capacity for school improvement. It identified ways stakeholders minimise challenges of context to drive and sustain school improvement. It identified distributed practices as vital in school improvement by considering collective input in vision-led activity, system development, educational leadership and networking. All facets of the work school stakeholders do make them agents of change. The next chapter, Chapter 4, considers the attribute of school culture in the capacity building process.

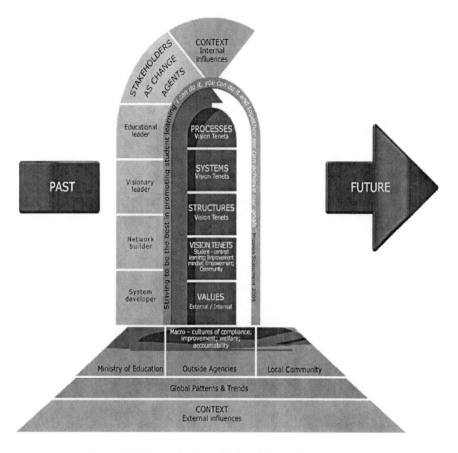

Figure 3.1 School Attribute: Stakeholders as Change Agents

NOTES

[xii] A school zone is a catchment area designated by the board of trustees and agreed to by the Ministry of Education from which the school can draw its pupils.

SCHOOL ATTRIBUTE

School Culture

Since the 1980s researchers have emphasised culture as a way of improving schools (Stoll, 1999; Hopkins et al. 1994). Mulford, Silins and Andrew (2003) contend that any or all school reforms are likely to fail in the face of cultural resistance. Daft (2002) advises that, when an organisations' culture is not in alignment with the needs of the external environment and the values and ways of doing things may reflect what worked in the past, cultural gaps occur making enactment and actualisation of reform doubtful. In fact, nothing schools do is actually culturally neutral (ERO, 2000). As Owens (1991) notes, "The culture of an organisation exerts powerful influence on … the way that participants perceive events and make sense of those events" (p. 175). Furthermore, "organisational culture is the body of solutions to problems that work consistently for a group and is therefore taught to new members as the correct way to perceive, think about, and feel in relation to those problems" (p. 204).

To understand the role culture plays in capacity building for school improvement, perceptions stakeholders have of school life need to be taken into consideration. Findings from this study suggest that culture is a social construct; a blended combination of history, macro and micro cultural values, beliefs and norms, current practice and aspirations of stakeholders. It is what Deal and Kennedy (1982; 1983) consider to be 'the way things are done around here'; that is, shared values that give rise to behavioural norms. In this school, 'the way things are around here' is linked to the school's vision, 'striving to be the best in promoting students learning' and the four tenets of student centred learning, improvement mindset, empowerment and community.

Chapter 4 starts by examining the way external and internal influences of context impact on the values, beliefs and norms of members to promote behaviour traits upheld as cultural hallmarks. Cultural hallmarks have implications for capacity building and improvement. They are constructed by stakeholders to represent the symbolic, practical and linguistic interactions in practice. Cultural hallmarks of significance are: collaboration; a learning culture; a culture of inclusion; commitment; and a safe place. In this chapter, each is defined in terms of key characteristics and contributions to capacity building for improvement. The chapter concludes by considering school culture and capacity building links.

EXTERNAL AND INTERNAL INFLUENCES ON COLLECTIVE VALUES, BELIEFS AND NORMS

External and internal environments emit particular values and beliefs to influence the work of stakeholders. A confluence of macro and micro values and beliefs create norms of behaviour that represent legitimate practice in a particular context. External influences of a macro context with influences on the collective values and beliefs of stakeholders in this school can be traced to Acts of Parliament, Ministry of Education legislation, outside agency input and local community needs and aspirations. For example, Ministry of Education policies that purport a strong central regulatory framework, devolved decision making, measurable outputs and quasi market influences are confirmed as emitting values of efficiency, prescribed compliance, accountability and improvement. Daily activity in this school or 'how things are done around here' adopts an approach that is characteristically rational and systemic. There is a valuing of efficiency, 'being strategic', and meeting regulatory demands within what is deemed reasonable. Macro cultural norms of compliance, accountability and improvement embedded in a belief system that values self-governance and self-management is articulated in the mission statement *I can do it, you can do it and together we can achieve our goals.*

As noted in Chapter 1, the Ministry of Education's improving schools rhetoric creates both opportunities and tensions in the policies advocated. For example, according to the Education Standards Act (2001), schools are expected to set targets for student achievement and monitor and report on progress in reaching them. Macro cultural norms of compliance and accountability continually imposed combined with a belief in 'improvement from within' (Barth, 1990) means target setting, achievement and monitoring of progress is taken seriously by all stakeholders. Apart from adhering to Ministry demands, stakeholders are driven towards promoting student learning, attracting the community back to the school, encouraging roll growth and dispelling past negative school perceptions. The notion advanced is that macro cultural norms of target setting, rewards and sanctions do not sufficiently explain or define what happens in this setting and rather, target setting and monitoring of progress is traceable to a learning community ethos and commitment to building capacity for improvement. In this site, compliance, accountability and improvement encompass a wider focus of building parent capacity and celebrating diversity. The stance is vision-led; that is, high levels of professionalism and work related practice get enacted in pursuit of 'striving to be the best in promoting student learning'.

The external influence of outside agencies on professional development also reflects dual attendance to fulfilling compliance and accountability requirements and, equally, development of a professional learning culture. Professional development that adheres strictly to Ministry of Education guidelines (for example, in addressing professional standards requirements) is considered compliance driven. Professional development of the kind that raises the quality of teaching and learning, stakeholder motivation and collective knowledge generation is referred to as commitment to learning and to a community of learners and leaders approach to school life. A community perspective is concerned with 'doing one's best in promoting student learning' in keeping with the vision and where the emphasis is placed on learning, inclusion, collaboration, commitment and a safe place - the key cultural hallmarks of this school.

Low socio-economic location factors have an impact on community perceptions of the school and perpetuate misconceptions. Comments such as, *they see multi-cultural faces and they think well they are obviously bullies* develops in stakeholders feelings of protectiveness, *but I would say we don't tolerate bullying...we don't tolerate disrespect of people or property and the children are taught to treat others as they want to be treated.* Challenges of setting prove binding elements that draw school stakeholders together. The kinship created promotes action in combating unjustified, negative labels. Values of fairness, non-racism, tolerance, respect, and togetherness or community are openly advocated. These values bind people to the school and to each other. Related to school culture, the following descriptions are made, *it's very warm and obviously very multicultural; we have richness here and we are proud of this. We cater for a very wide variety of needs;* and *you've got to be positive and fair.*

The school's vision counts as an internal influence on the culture. For example, the statement that, *most teachers' goals are to improve children's achievement, you know, emotional and social well being as well* places an emphasis on the holistic nature of schooling and student-centred learning. Vision cannot, in itself, explain school culture. Culture requires inquiry into the social side of practice; that is, reciprocity of influence of people on one another and on practice.

Personal attributes of school stakeholders act as binding elements of culture. The following comments acknowledge attributes considered crucial and that have a bearing on the culture: *being friendly, getting on. Everybody shares what they have got;* and *there are people on the staff who haven't got negative attitudes.* Much admired personal attributes are those of sharing, being friendly, positive and getting along. In as much as these are desirable personal attributes, there are also those considered unacceptable, *narrow minded people, those lacking in tolerance and who are judgemental.*

All senior managers in this school are women and their presence reportedly influences the school's culture in terms of management style considered collaborative and less hierarchical:

> *This is the first time that we have had a woman as a principal. This is good for us as female teachers looking at her as role models of women so we can achieve ... coming from my culture and the hierarchy you can't question the men about things. Now if we have something we do not understand we ask ... the culture of this school has changed since the women took over. We know we respect them; the principal treats you like an adult, a professional, like somebody that she trusts. She doesn't belittle you. She respects you.*

Changes in community demographics are internal factors that have and continue to influence school culture. Changing community demographics[xiii] means that *the children's culture ends up being the school's culture.* Students influence the culture of the school. For example, past inappropriate student behaviour created a dysfunctional culture where staff members worked in isolation with very little by way of collaboration or community. Such thoughts remain fresh in people's mind even though the school's situation has improved. Past memories create a drive to ensure safety and promote this school as a 'safe place'. In response to avoiding past behaviour patterns returning, being prepared, organised, vigilant and exercising care and support have become embedded norms that engender and sustain a safe place ethos. A systemic approach, expectations of acceptable behaviour and peer support promote trust, collegiality, inclusion, commitment and learning.

This school's recent turbulent history has a more subtle influence on school culture. Statements such as, *two years back each one was not very free to share things or ideas* are recalled by staff with past school connections. Apart from establishing an understanding of why this school experienced a decline, past recollections offer guidance of how to avoid such events reoccurring. Acknowledging and appreciating the past strengthens in stakeholders the resolve to ensure future school success. It creates a culture that is improvement orientated: *I wouldn't call it a stagnant school.*

External and internal conditions of context influence the culture of the school. They establish values, beliefs and norms that legitimise action within constraints and freedom of this setting. The culture of this school is described as: *rich, caring, supportive, professional and exciting; positive and encouraging; vibrant and forward thinking; comfortable and collaborative.* The five cultural hallmarks prominent in practice contributing towards capacity building for school improvement include collaboration, a learning culture, a culture of inclusion, commitment, and a safe place. Each is described next from the viewpoint of key characteristics and contributions to capacity building for improvement.

HALLMARK: COLLABORATION

In environments that push for reform, collaborative cultures appear promising in initiating and sustaining school improvement. Hopkins et al. (1994) denote collaborative cultures as facilitating teacher development through mutual support, joint work and broad agreement on educational values. Further, collaborative cultures provide a way of minimising problems associated with individualism, balkanisation and contrived collegiality. Nias, Southworth and Yeomans (1989) on collaborative work arrangements comment that, "the relationships which they create are tough and flexible enough to withstand shocks and uncertainties from within and without" (p. 74). Hargreaves (1991, cited in Hopkins et al. 1994) describes collaborative cultures as:

- Spontaneous: emerging from teachers themselves as a social group;
- Voluntary: relationships are valued for the experience, fun and productive ways of working;
- Development oriented: capable of initiating change by working on externally supported or mandated initiatives to which there is allegiance;

– Pervasive across time and space: through "passing words and glances, praise and thanks, offers to exchange classes in tough times, suggestions about new ideas, informal discussions about new units, sharing problems or meeting parents together" (p. 94); and

– Unpredictable: The outcomes are often uncertain and not easily predicted which makes collaborative cultures incompatible in school systems that are highly centralised.

In this school, collaboration is defined as: *working together as a team from the hierarchy down to the scale 'A' teachers*. Collaboration has various meanings open to interpretation. For staff, collaboration necessitates team building, having fun and appreciating togetherness. Opportunities for team building are woven into the fabric of school life, *we get along on Friday afternoons. There's that sense of humour ... It is a family thing. That's the core of it all it's a family. Like it doesn't matter if you have your inadequacies, you're accepted in the family*. A family metaphor, openly articulated, necessitates the giving of self for others, working for the betterment of all, pursuit of vision ideals and sharing in the development of a school community. Parents associate it with loyalty and emotional ties of attachment to the school. To act in collaboration means working for the common good from a position that enforces community. Collaboration is seen to build trust defined as: *if you say something it won't be held against you, your opinion is valued, what you do is recognised and as a person you're respected*. Trust related to sharing knowledge and task accomplishment means, *you are just standing there chit chatting and then someone will say it has been really hard and then someone will pop up and say have you tried this or I'll give you a hand*. Collaboration and trust promote goodwill which works to sustain passion and commitment in working towards vision.

HALLMARK: A LEARNING CULTURE

Current thought on organisational learning is that knowledge and skills of teachers can be increased through collegial opportunities to solve problems through collective dialogue (Fullan & Miscall, 2000). This, Fullan and Miscall suggest, requires a "collective approach to learning, throughout a school, or even school system" (p. 34). The value of collective dialogue in changing teacher practice and improving student achievement is well substantiated by the literature highlighting the value of a learning culture where conversations compel teachers to focus on evaluating and improving their own and others' practice in cultures that encourage analysis and critique (see for example Annan, Lai & Robinson, 2003; Timperley & Robinson, 2001; Symes, Jeffries, Timperley, & Lai, 2001; Phillips, McNaughton, & MacDonald, 2001). A learning culture is defined by Kilgore (1999) as, "not only a concept of the group as a learner and constructor of knowledge but, also, an understanding of the centrality of the group's vision of social justice that drives it to act" (p. 191). Such ideas are useful frames by which to consider the nature and type of behaviours that identify 'a learning culture' as a hallmark that builds capacity for improvement.

In this school, norms of learning are deeply embedded in school culture and inform the way things are done around here. Learning, regarded as *useful, relevant and tied to goal achievement*, encourages a work ethic that means: *Things are happening in my class now, I can see progress.* Internal (colleagues) and external (outside agencies) support from 'positions of consistency' enhances the learning culture. Positions of consistency mean assistance, if requested, is provided. Unlimited support, collaboration and trust in people, systems, processes and structures to deliver, account for comments such as, *I think if you don't trust the people with whom you're working with or with whom you have issues then it's very hard to learn.* A culture of learning in this school is considered inspirational and contagious. In this setting, learning expands to meet parents' requirements. Home-school partnerships and parent chat sessions encourage parental involvement in education and school life.

HALLMARK: A CULTURE OF INCLUSION

Participants claim supporting other cultures is not new but something of a tradition. Furthermore, this school reflects bi-culturalism and multi-culturalism. I think it is important to be bi-cultural and then multi-cultural. Tangata whenua[xiv] has status and it is not just because the Treaty says but we live and breathe it. The statement, Tangata whenua has status depicts a deep sense of respect for Maori people and their tikanga.[xv] For example, "before Nga Ringa Awhina[xvi] was moved, the tapu[xvii] had to be lifted. The ground that Nga Ringa Awhina was moved to had to be blessed and the first breaking of the soil was done at the same time.

Support for bi-culturalism and multi-culturalism goes beyond celebration of culture through song and dance. Support taps into systems, processes and structures to advance cultural values of respect, tolerance, non-racism, care and compassion and community. To illustrate, bi-lingual tutor assistance in providing support for parents with limited English, *gives them opportunities to talk ... Those parents really need to know what the children are learning and should feel that they are part of the school too.* Respect for people of other ethnicities is actively promoted and supported by staff in the creation of an inclusive school environment where, *there is an after school programme for the Ethiopian children and the school is used for adult education programmes.* Staff support for home-school partnership programmes and parent chat sessions are other forms of parental support. Home-school partnerships, for example, involve school staff assisting parents to lead their own community members in matters of education. A culture of inclusion and support is traceable to the school's vision necessitating: *valuing of culture and diversity and celebration of success. It's all interwoven and so it develops into this positive approach to developing learners for the future.*

HALLMARK: COMMITMENT

In this school, staff and parents are prepared to go the extra mile if it means 'striving to be the best in promoting student learning'. For staff with past school association, commitment is linked to loyalty: *This has been my only school. I've done my training. I've done some relieving. I was volunteering in this school.* Parents' commitment is associated with this being their local school, *I mean if it is your local school you can't say there are too many unsavoury children there and I don't like the colour of their skin too. If you live in the place then you send your kids to the local school.* There is open expressed loyalty to the school and loyalty linked to commitment means giving of self in ways that benefit the school and those associated with it.

Commitment is associated with hard work. Comments such as, *staff are very dedicated and they work long hours* abound. In achieving school turnaround, staff recall, *I know the staff as a whole have come together and they work really hard.* Messages of, *the more you practice the better you get* are repeated frequently by individuals and groups. Working hard is a shared group norm; *it's the attitude that if it's good enough for them (senior management) then it's good enough for us.*

Commitment is connected to empowerment; more particularly to expression of voice and knowing it will be heard and enacted. Voice is connected with 'ownership' (individual and collective). Examples of ownership abound around here. For example, with respect to vision evolution, the comment made was, *things are taken on board by the leaders and the feeling is we have a say in things.* By way of another example, setting up an environmental-friendly school was said to originate from a team decision but spread to encompass the whole school, *it was just in our team we were talking about this when a teacher mentioned it to the principal. Now we are already thinking about the garden and changing the school environment.* Decisions made on future teaching topics provide yet another example of commitment in the form of curriculum collaborative decision-making. Decisions reached through collaboration and negotiation foster team spirit.

Commitment is a by-product of trust seen here as an expectation that others can and will help if asked. Here, the notion of reciprocity is strong: *The principal and deputy principal support their staff and because they do that the staff will support them. Teachers know that if they have problems or need help, the supports are there for them; The (principal) was always there to listen and help*; and, *In a traditional school, teacher aides are not held in much esteem but here, teacher aides play a vital role in school turnaround.*

HALLMARK: A SAFE PLACE

The value placed on 'feeling safe' has links to this school's past where limited support and feelings of teacher isolation created a dysfunctional culture. Staff feelings of safety are now captured as: *They are always there for us* and *I like things structured; if I was to go and say to the deputy principal look I'm struggling here, things would be put in place to give me a hand*; and *we don't get double messages.* Parents' feelings of safety result from having knowledge, *parents know the teachers and know what's going on and that's the whole point of home-school partnership.*

Learning and feeling safe are linked. For example, participation in Ministry of Education professional development contracts means, *teams working together* and *teachers coming together and working on things to build their confidence.* Working in teams is observed as providing individualised learning support. However, there is also an expectation that movement beyond team boundaries is necessary in reducing dependency, *you have to do it for yourself.* Feeling safe within team boundaries builds confidence to traverse outside it to take risks and increase self-efficacy.

School systems, processes and structures of accountability promote the school as a 'safe place'. They endorse purpose and growth that benefits students, parents and staff learning. Staff collaboration in planning and delivery of the curriculum contributes towards a 'safe place': *We make sure we organise our planning and our resources for each lesson*; and, as observed by a parent, *Every morning I just walk inside and everything is already organised. As soon as it's 9.00 a.m. teachers sit and call the roll and everything is ready for the kids.* Attention to detail equates to an organised, structured school environment. The climate endorsed is one of organised work: *I like it structured in a proper way*; and *In this school the procedures are in place and people know exactly where they stand and what's expected. I think clarity, expectation, follow through and support for teachers are important.*

Systems of communication facilitate a managed, structured approach to school life. They bring people on board, build cohesion and create a sense of security claimed as, *when things are happening they do tell us and so all of us know the same thing.* Communication systems facilitate information flow. To illustrate, the school's whiteboard in the staff room acts as a tool for transmitting messages of daily and weekly importance. Everyone shares in the recording of messages. The whiteboard is a cultural symbol of this school representative of individuals functioning within a community.

Feeling safe is connected to learning and is the result of supportive school practices and senior staff working towards meeting individual needs as captured by these comments, *they are not expecting someone with basic skills to work at high levels; There is an allowance for you to develop at your own pace, to hook into programmes with your children according to your ability and level of development. There is flexibility to make the professional development fit your needs.* Furthermore, voluntary help, specialist support, peer and teacher aide assistance provides additional support for teachers wanting to initiate change of practice. In-built support alleviates teacher isolation or long hours spent alone in the classroom. Help from parents, teacher aides, bi-lingual workers and specialist staff members provide safety-nets of support for teachers on a daily basis.

SCHOOL CULTURE: CAPACITY BUILDING LINKS

In this school there are five cultural hallmarks with direct links to capacity building for school improvement. The cultural hallmarks are manifestations of culture that enhance professionalism and social cohesion acknowledged as *this is a place where children and teachers want to be and want to learn.* High levels of professionalism and social cohesion create a 'safe' place ethos conducive to building capacity for improvement.

A 'safe' place provides bridging and buffering zones that guard against challenges of context that may disrupt individual, collective and systemic equilibrium. Equally important and connected to the notion of a 'safe' place are forces that encourage stepping outside zones of comfort to push the boundaries of learning. Group norms of collaboration and learning, commitment and inclusivity builds trust which sustains behaviour directed towards building capacity for school improvement.

Conversations in this school support the vision ideal of 'striving to be the best in promoting student learning'. According to the principal, *the talk has changed over the years. They were always moaning because there were behaviour problems and now in the staff room you do not hear moans and groans. The attitudes of staff have changed to one of professionalism.* Professionalism, the result of an interweaving of all cultural hallmarks means engagement in change of practice to promote capacity for improvement.

The culture of this school is friendly, supportive, collaborative, learning orientated and professional. This means, *you feel like you are all doing the job together, helping each other out. It's not like you're isolated just working away in your own classroom.* School stakeholders endorse the collective values, beliefs and norms as evidenced by the following comments, *we really are trying to work together; we do share ideas in our teams; we try to understand each other; and we are working well.* In this school allegiance to school values and beliefs indicates a cohesive school culture where everyone pulls in the same direction.

Cultural hallmarks in this school are observable. They contribute to feelings of wellness and positivity. A positive, safe environment promotes energy and altruism, essential qualities that facilitate capacity building for school improvement.

CONCLUSION

Culture has a major impact on people and their ability to undertake improvement related activities. In this school there is acknowledgement of diversity and a willingness to incorporate all stakeholders in creating an inclusive, professional learning community. Here, being part of a 'family' means the school is considered supportive, inclusive and empowering of all stakeholders. Cultural hallmarks reduce anxiety often associated with change. The potential for conflict and misunderstanding is minimised because of the stance taken in collectively maximising curriculum delivery, building relationships and encouraging home-school partnerships. Working towards greater parent involvement in school life is an attempt to counteract some of the barriers ethnic minority groups face. This school's culture is influenced by macro and micro cultural norms, current school practice, history and people associated with the school. A blending of all creates a fertile ground within which to construct and enact processes that build capacity for school improvement.

Figure 4.1 captures the essential hallmarks of this school's culture. As an attribute of capacity building, school culture is added to the central component of vision denoting a strong correspondence to it. Linkage with the aforementioned attribute of stakeholders as change agents is also reinforced in positioning school culture on the 'other' side of vision. In the next chapter, Chapter 5, professional development as the fourth and final attribute is explicated.

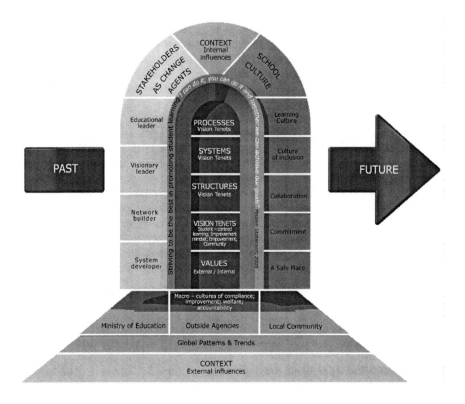

Figure 4.1 School Attribute: School Culture

NOTES

[xiii] NZ European/Pākehā 16%, Samoan 14%, Māori 10%, Tongan 11%, Indian 11%, Ethiopian 6%, Somalian 5%, Niuean 4%, Cook Island 4%, Other 19% (ERO, 2005).
[xiv] Tangata whenua is indigenous people of New Zealand.
[xv] Tikanga – customs; rules; principles; obligations; conditions (legal); and provisions (legal).

[xvi] Nga Ringa – Maori translation – helping hands. As explained by one school stakeholder, Nga Ringa Awhina is a building that was used to house teaching resources for Maori. Since its change of location, Maori resources are now stored in a central resource area. The building is planned to be used in different ways.
[xvii] Tapu – sacred.

SCHOOL ATTRIBUTE

Professional Development

Professional development initiated in this setting is profuse, complex and intricately interwoven into the fabric of school life. It proceeds in a developmental, incremental, integrated and continuous manner – a layered approach. External factors of influence stem from the Ministry of Education, outside agencies,[xviii] tertiary institutions, business sector interests, networking with schools, overseas connections, professional associations and access to educational websites such as Te Kete Ipurangi (TKI).[xix] Internal factors of influence relate to what happens in practice in terms of collaborative interchange, reflective practice and openness to new ideas. Management of professional development in related to flexibility, relevance and scaffolded learning also exert influence. Combined, such influences generate what I term collaborative professional development that leads to purpose driven learning.[xx] Professional development is situated at the external/internal interface of the capacity building model (see Figure 5.2) justified on the basis that knowledge is both internally and externally sourced. In this chapter, the discussion on professional development as an attribute of capacity building for school improvement is presented according to:

– External factors of influence;
– Internal factors of influence;
– A layered approach; and
– Capacity building links.

EXTERNAL FACTORS OF INFLUENCE

External influences on professional development highlight source, choice and outcomes rather than detailing a particular intervention. Delimiting the scope in such a manner is justified on the basis that what is presented helps paint a holistic picture of professional development as a layered approach. External sources of professional development relate to the Ministry of Education, outside agencies, tertiary and business sector influences, networking with other schools, overseas connections, professional associations and taping into the educational web sites.

Ministry of Education

Findings from this study indicate that meeting legislative requirements has an influence on professional development. For example, updating staff knowledge on Ministry of Education compliance measures increases legislative knowledge and ensures system, structure and curriculum delivery fit with *The National Education Guidelines*. This aspect of professional development is seen to traverse across school levels (board, staff, team and curriculum development) where Ministry of Education professional requirements are discussed and enacted to ensure school systems, processes and structures meet current legislative demands.

Meeting regulatory demands forms an obligatory part of professional learning. Here, the principal disseminates knowledge acquired by, *being aware of what's going on, by reading and attending local cluster principal's meetings and keeping informed of Ministry developments*. The benefits of this for the individual, collective and system include:

- Increased compliance and legislative knowledge;
- Holistic attendance to meeting student needs;
- Systemic change that achieves alignment to government mandates and
- Creation of a school environment considered a 'safe place'.

In the year of data collection, the following Ministry contracts served as sources for professional input:

- Numeracy Professional Development Projects – Early Numeracy Project (ENP) mainly undertaken in 2003 and Advanced Numeracy Project (ANP)[xxi] in 2004;
- Information and Communication Technology (ICT);[xxii]
- Parent Mentoring Initiative – Home / School Partnership program;[xxiii] and
- English Literacy Assistant Course[xxiv] (ELA) for teacher aides.

Outside Agencies

The influence of outside agencies on professional development is complex and linked to numerous facets of school life resulting in:

- Systemic, individual and collective learning;
- Change in practice;
- Networking with others; and
- Opportunities to engage in professional dialogue on practice.

As facilitative agents, outside agencies work in spaces that build relationships: between the Ministry and the school; senior management and staff; staff and students; staff and parents; and staff, parents and students. Their knowledge, expertise and people skills award them credibility to enact change. The positive influence of outside agencies on professional development is legitimised for several reasons: depth of specialist knowledge; expertise and ability to provide objective assessment of need; construction of action plans in response; enactment of plans to improve practice; and input which may be the only course of support available in situations where site knowledge and expertise are limited. Professional development by outside agencies influences the building of individual and collective knowledge in curriculum and pedagogy as pre-entry assessment, professional input based on need and exit points adjusted to organisational 'fit' have the potential to build individual, collective and systemic knowledge capacities.

Tertiary

Tertiary sources of influence are not just limited to staff access to 'formal' study at university. They extend to one day courses *if it is in line with what people's needs and interests are*. Such *room to manoeuvre* is rationalised as *bringing things back into the school* and positively affecting individual, collective and systemic learning aimed at improvement. In addition, tertiary influences on staff learning occur indirectly through, for example, partnership with universities in teacher training programmes and the benefits of such relationships mean *it's good to see the new teachers coming out of college with new strategies and for us to look at them and to observe their new ways instead of focusing on the old ways.*

Business Sector

Business sector influences are another source of professional development. Motivation for this comes from the principal who is described as *always looking for new ideas*. The value staff award to this source of new learning relates to increased pedagogical and content knowledge, transference of newly acquired knowledge to promote student learning and communal sharing of ideas that builds confidence in curriculum delivery. Sponsoring and implementation of the 'You Can Do It' programme is an example of a purchased resource with business sector links. In this school, principles underpinning the programme proved instrumental in establishing school identity captured in the mission statement *I can do it, you can do it and together we can achieve our goals.*

Networking with Other Schools

Networking with other schools is not undertaken randomly but remains specific to purpose. As a form of professional development, networking with schools promotes a, *filtering through of information* to benefit stakeholders. Individual benefit is reportedly job specific. The principal, for example, stated she remained 'current' by *attending local cluster principals' meetings and the larger Auckland principals' meetings on aspects of curriculum delivery*. Similarly, teachers acknowledged an increase of curriculum and pedagogical knowledge through networking with other schools. Networks for learning can be linked to individual or collective development.

Participation in Ministry contracts creates opportunities for networking with other schools also participating in the contract. The ICT contract, for example, enabled staff to visit schools *to look at class newsletters and to find some useful web sites*. Networking, in this case, was facilitator dependent and trust in the facilitator to establish networks that are aligned with the vision of the school was acknowledged as enhancing learning. Staff initiated networks are aligned to school-wide goals designed to achieve purpose.

Overseas Connections

In the year of data collection, the principal and ICT coordinator attended an ICT conference in Brisbane, Australia. The deputy principal attended a principals' conference in Melbourne, Australia. Engagement in such international professional development meetings provides an expanded take on education. They promote wider networks that support growth. New knowledge is also introduced by overseas educators visiting the school. International knowledge exchange adds to a climate where 'openness to new ideas' is encouraged.

Professional Associations

Senior managers and staff are affiliated members of various professional associations. Staff claim professional associations provide networks of support. Involvement has distinct advantages in terms of building individual, collective and systemic capacity for improvement. For example:
- Internal and external networks are regarded crucial in maintaining currency of practice;
- Current information, brought back to the school, is of collective benefit; and
- Information gained ensures this school sustains its position at the cutting edge of knowledge development.

Educational Websites

Access to educational websites (observed in staff and team meetings) occur in relation to collaborative planning and consolidation of new learning. Tapping into government procured educational websites reinforces this expansive attitude to knowledge production and utilisation. At joint planning sessions (team and whole school) communal sharing of internet information was observed as building a collective knowledge pool that brings people together. Outside facilitators add to this generic pool of knowledge. Ease of access to computers and shared knowledge of suitable educational websites encourage staff to gain and distribute information freely. This adds to existing layers of knowledge in the school which foster 'openness to new ideas' and knowledge flow across all levels of the school.

INTERNAL FACTORS OF INFLUENCE

In this school, vision tenets underpin the professional development agenda. Vision tenets advance buy-in to practices such as collaborative interchange, reflective practice and openness to new ideas which serve as forms of professional development. Aspects of management in regard to professional development such as flexibility, relevance and scaffolded learning are also considered influential internal determinants.

Collaborative Interchange

Collaborative interchange is defined as *sharing things, learning from each other ... like if you have any problems you can go to the senior management for support.* Collaborative interchange facilitates team work: planning together, sharing knowledge, collective learning and building a learning culture. Team work is common practice[xxv] in this environment. Division of the school into teams[xxvi] promotes teamness described as *within our team meetings it's a time we can talk about different things we can teach different ways of managing children.* Professional development undertaken in teams establishes an eclectic knowledge base. An eclectic knowledge base includes knowledge of students, community and staff, an understanding of school systems, processes and structures, and curriculum, pedagogical and legislative knowledge. Eclectic knowledge enhances:
- Shared responsibility of pedagogical change aligned to school/stakeholder needs;
- Knowledge use that maximises curriculum delivery;
- Creation of a substantial knowledge base for framing, making and taking decisions;
- Connectedness among stakeholders attributed to a pool of collective knowledge;
- Renewal of systems, processes and structures to ensure systemic coherence; and
- Affirmation of norms of improvement, learning, empowerment and community focused on 'striving to be the best in promoting student learning'.

In this setting, collaborative interchange promotes positive working relationships. It develops an environment of collegial trust. Trust encourages reflective practice and critique of practice as this comment implies, *the tutor teacher would give me lots of assistance. She would observe my lessons and give me feedback... I could always go and ask her for ideas and suggestions.* A product of collaboration and trust is risk taking and/or pushing the boundaries of individual and collective learning. Participants claim learning is empowering as *teachers are encouraged to take on board a new project or a new idea and it might be something that's never been tried before. They are given a chance to have a go at it.* Collaborative interchange, trust and risk taking builds self-efficacy acknowledged as *we book ourselves in if we are interested in learning and we set goals for the kids to improve but now we have our own goals.* Benefits equate to:
- Individualised learning;
- Engagement in continuous professional development;
- Reflection on practice;
- Experimentation with new teaching strategies; and
- Self-monitoring and tracking of progress.

Reflective Practice

In this setting, reflection on practice engenders professional learning. It is defined by staff as: *You evaluate what you're doing and measure it against the new*

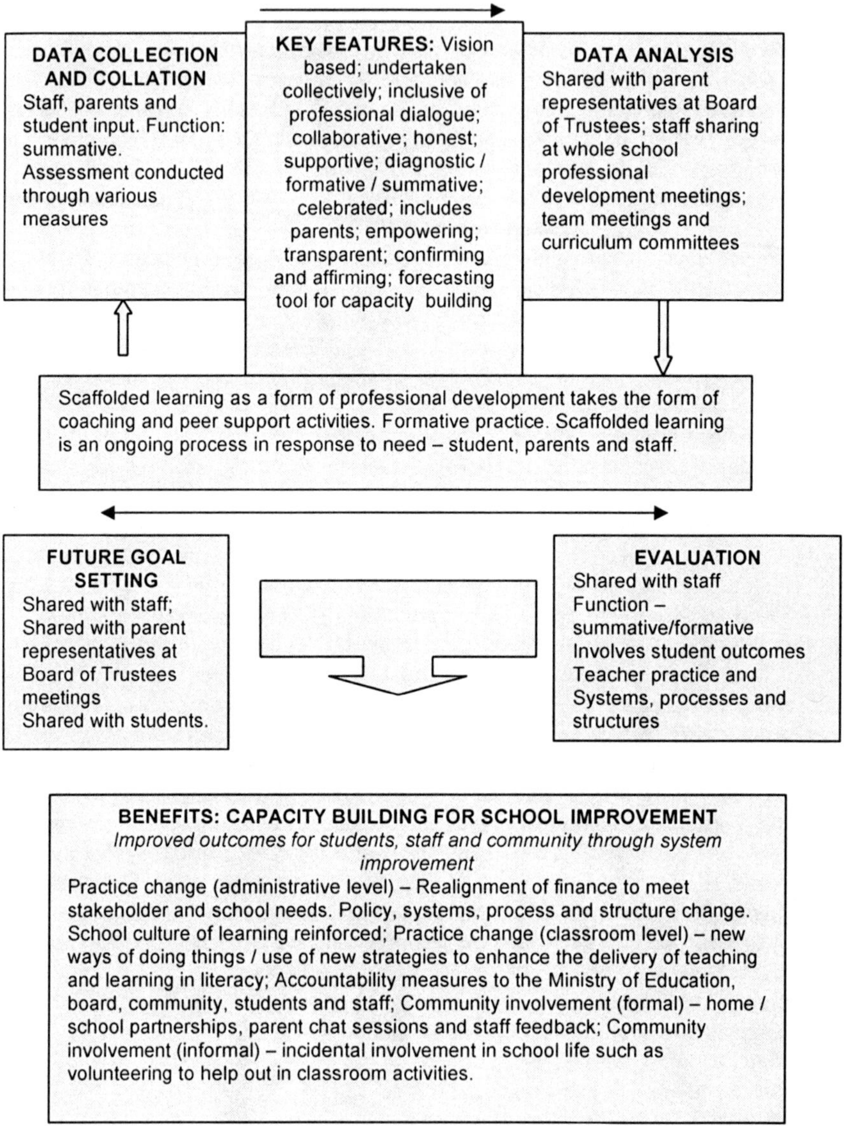

DATA COLLECTION AND COLLATION
Staff, parents and student input. Function: summative. Assessment conducted through various measures

KEY FEATURES: Vision based; undertaken collectively; inclusive of professional dialogue; collaborative; honest; supportive; diagnostic / formative / summative; celebrated; includes parents; empowering; transparent; confirming and affirming; forecasting tool for capacity building

DATA ANALYSIS
Shared with parent representatives at Board of Trustees; staff sharing at whole school professional development meetings; team meetings and curriculum committees

Scaffolded learning as a form of professional development takes the form of coaching and peer support activities. Formative practice. Scaffolded learning is an ongoing process in response to need – student, parents and staff.

FUTURE GOAL SETTING
Shared with staff; Shared with parent representatives at Board of Trustees meetings Shared with students.

EVALUATION
Shared with staff Function – summative/formative Involves student outcomes Teacher practice and Systems, processes and structures

BENEFITS: CAPACITY BUILDING FOR SCHOOL IMPROVEMENT
Improved outcomes for students, staff and community through system improvement
Practice change (administrative level) – Realignment of finance to meet stakeholder and school needs. Policy, systems, process and structure change. School culture of learning reinforced; Practice change (classroom level) – new ways of doing things / use of new strategies to enhance the delivery of teaching and learning in literacy; Accountability measures to the Ministry of Education, board, community, students and staff; Community involvement (formal) – home / school partnerships, parent chat sessions and staff feedback; Community involvement (informal) – incidental involvement in school life such as volunteering to help out in classroom activities.

Figure 5.1 Reading Review

strategies and you adapt it; You see the parts that are valuable and are still valued;and, I think it is about talking, discussing and trying things out and then doing some reviews and finding out where we are at and what we are going to do to improve.

Reflection on practice is a renewal process desirous of improvement. As the comments below indicate, it attaches meaning to work and ensuing debate provides opportunities to scrutinise and alter practice:

We discuss how we are going to take the piece of writing, what we are looking for and how we are going to standardise the writing and how we are going to moderate it ... in doing so we need professional development on using the exemplars and what's out there to help us in the job of moderating and working out where we are at.

In terms of value, the comment made was, none of us has all the answers. We are learning to respect someone else's viewpoint. Sometimes it strengthens the views you already hold. Reflection on practice produces a readiness to be critical, you have to be teachable as well and there is always another way of doing it. There is always something new that you can give the children. As seen in Figure 5.1, reflection facilitates felt need for change, creates 'openness to new ideas' and provides opportunities to alter practice in response to authenticated need.

Openness to New Ideas

'Openness to new ideas' is not mandated practice. It is a state of mind that exists in connection with learning. 'Openness to new ideas' sits comfortably alongside collaborative interchange and reflection on practice as internal sources of professional development. In this setting, a 'wanting to learn' attitude prevails. Behaviours that denote this include: welcoming outside expert' input, volunteering to attend professional development courses and association meetings, involvement in Ministry contracts and networking with other schools. Peer support, modelling, coaching, self evaluation and collective critique of practice are internal processes that sustain professional dialogue and 'openness to new ideas'.

MANAGEMENT OF PROFESSIONAL DEVELOPMENT: FLEXIBILITY

Collaborative interchange, reflective practice and openness to new ideas establish group norms of 'how things are done around here'. Such characteristics require professional development that displays *room to manoeuvre*; in other words, management of professional development that displays flexibility of design is important. Flexibility, at the system level, is evident in alterations to the professional development agenda in response to need. One such example observed was a professional development meeting on spelling. Input by the deputy principal was provided in direct response to staff request. Another example is flexibility shown at individual levels of professional development in terms of negotiation and control of learning as these comments imply: *You are not expected to take on board new thinking all in one hit. There is time to put things into place and take on board the parts that suit you and not fit completely into someone else's mode*; and *There are allowances for you to develop at your own pace and hook into the*

programmes with your children according to your ability and your level of development. Benefits from such flexibility mean:
– System and structure realignment in response to need (individual, collective and system);
– Learning that is highly meaningful and relevant for the learner; and
– Empowerment of learning by managing change. In an environment where change is constant, inserted flexibility is seen to reduce individual stress.

MANAGEMENT OF PROFESSIONAL DEVELOPMENT: RELEVANCY

Participants claim this school is a busy place, *constantly striving for improvement.* For professional development to be successful, staff claim it has to be, *relevant. I find if it is not relevant you just sit there and get absolutely bored.* Relevancy is defined as, *something you can take and use in your classroom or in your classroom practice. So it has to be at the right level and that sort of thing. I prefer it if it's practical.* Relevant professional development is:
– Meaningful: Conducted in a meaningful way;
– Incremental and progressive: *Like last year and this year there has been a focus on literacy;*
– Practical, for example in the Numeracy contract: *We have hands on activities. The booklets are really good guides. They are so self explanatory. There are lesson, unit plans, knowledge activities and teaching strategies; and, giving you ideas to try and implement in the class;*
– Achievable: *Things are happening in my class and I can see progress. It has helped us to work with our guided reading organisation to group and regroup the class. I think that the children are moving along very well;*
– Hands on or learning by doing: *Yeah it is better for you to actually learn by doing it. Like when we had an art staff meeting we actually did art. And then once you do it you sort of remember it; and, my learning is now learning on the job and that's the only way I can learn. If I get faced with a problem I either work it out for myself or enlist help or pass it on to someone I know who can help;*
– Inclusive of parents: *Parents help us in the class which is fantastic and they help our learning in many ways;* and
– Facilitative of professional dialogue.

MANAGEMENT OF PROFESSIONAL DEVELOPMENT: SCAFFOLDED LEARNING

Scaffolded learning is an on-going, continuous part of professional development. It is provided in response to stakeholder and systemic need and traceable to formal (reviews and appraisals) and informal (individual requests) systems of reflective practice. Scaffolded learning extends to parents engagement in home-school partnership activities and regular weekly parent chat sessions. Ministry initiatives, such as professional development training for newly appointed board members, scaffolds board learning in the area of governance.

Scaffolded learning connects directly to practice and is inclusive of individual and collective exchange of ideas. It necessitates the asking of 'hard questions'. In the initial stages of school improvement, the principal's 'hard questions' related to pedagogy which meant she, *talked and interviewed teachers about how they felt about the reading programme. She discussed what they were doing.* Hard questions force staff to confront reality. They have the potential to raise doubt as to the appropriateness of practice that exists. Scaffolded learning creates a culture of reflective practice, collaborative interchange and 'openness to new ideas'.

The asking of 'hard questions' continues to be common practice in this school, occurring at junction points where stakeholders meet to discuss learning and teaching needs and future school direction. The asking of 'hard questions' has the potential to move inquiry of practice past surface levels of understanding to a deeper consideration of purpose and authenticity as revealed by the data. The courage shown by staff to engage in such rigorous analysis of data establishes accurate starting points for learning and change of practice. Scaffolded learning, thus conceived, is an evidence-driven activity with a foothold in reality.

Scaffolded learning promotes ongoing networks of support, collaboration with peers and/or outside agencies. Peer and/or expert knowledge, expertise and skills are essential in the development of an incremental, integrated, layered approach to professional development. Systemic levels of support, provided by the school and other sources like the Ministry, enhance scaffolded learning in this school. School policies, systems of performance management, staff induction and reviews support and endorse scaffolded learning as a form of professional development.

A LAYERED APPROACH

Professional development in this school is layered. This is the result of:
- Formal and planned meetings;
- Informal, unplanned opportunities for knowledge exchange; and
- Monitored practice.

Layered Approach: Formal/Planned

Whole staff professional development meetings occur weekly. The staff room and individual classrooms serve as venues for such meetings. Meetings held in classrooms provide incidental opportunities for learning confirmed as, *we move around people's classrooms not to check up on them but for everybody to get new ideas and see things and this makes people feel important too and everyone is recognised by their colleagues.*

Weekly staff meetings last an hour to an hour and a half. Although there is a set agenda, there are also times when alterations and/or additions are made to suit need. Professional development is linked to the overall school's focus as detailed in the strategic plan. Staff note, *so there are things that we'll look at throughout the year, focuses we'll have and so then they're up and everyone gets the instruction on like guided reading, or reciprocal reading, three level guides that sort of thing.*

Knowledge introduced at staff meetings is a mixture of theory and practice modified to suit context. Information introduced at whole school staff meetings is reinforced at team meetings. Here, ideas and concepts undergo further adjustment and modification to suit student age level requirements. Whole staff and team meetings create opportunities for individual and collective learning. School based knowledge expands to include the community. Parents are kept informed of educational developments via newsletters, home-school partnership evenings and parent chat sessions.

An additional aspect of a layered approach is transmission of new knowledge from sources outside the school. Such transference is initiated when staff attend out of school courses, return with knowledge to share and modify and enact new learning accordingly. External transfer of information means new knowledge enters the school and is subsequently dispersed through stakeholder involvement. The responsibility for knowledge acquisition, dissemination and implementation is the responsibility of all staff. Shared responsibility for learning leads to a collective knowledge base and a community of leaders approach to knowledge production and utilisation. Social processing of knowledge enhances a culture of learning.

External input of a more specific kind enters the school in response to agency requests for help and support relative to individual, collective and/or systemic need. Such input also has an expansive, layered quality which benefits both the individual who made the request, the collective and/or the system. For example, knowledge requested by an individual staff member in response to a particular student, quickly becomes communal property in an environment where knowledge sharing is encouraged. The same can be said of infrastructures of support in response to planned intervention. The holistic nature of information and support provided by outside agencies goes beyond focused attention on the curriculum. Information giving extends to social, emotional and behavioural aspects of whole child development.

Formal, planned and layered professional development has the potential to motivate and sustain learning. In terms of capacity building for school improvement, benefits include:

– Establishment of external and internal networks of support for learning;
– Modification of external knowledge to suit site conditions with potential to enhance change of practice;
– Shared responsibility for knowledge production and utilisation;
– Norms of learning, empowerment and improvement embedded in school culture; and
– Creation and expansion of an eclectic knowledge base with potential to enhance practice and inform decision-making.

Layered Approach: Unplanned/Informal

In this setting, learning occurs through unplanned, informal conversations held spontaneously. According to the deputy principal, *professional dialogue happens and sometimes it's quite informal. You know it might be an informal thing in the staff room. It's a sharing of ideas. I constantly have people coming in and that's part of professional development for staff.*

Informal conversations serve to reinforce and clarify aspects of daily activity. They are, as one staff member notes, *a lot of incidental stuff and they'll say hey look I've found out about this or do this.* Informal conversations or teacher talk are a product of collaboration. Their value lies in reinforcing patterns of workplace behaviours and shared values. In a sense, unplanned informal conversations are 'sense making' activities that reinforce group ways of working. They help establish group identity which, in this setting, offers opportunity to develop a learning community.

Monitored Practice

Professional development is taken seriously in this school. By its very nature, it reflects the complexities inherent in building capacity for school improvement. Taking professional development seriously involves monitoring and evaluating new learning that occurs as *it's all about improving staff skills and then monitoring what happens within the classrooms as well.* Monitored practice is seen as accountability to self, colleagues, students, parents and the Ministry of Education as in reporting on requirements as stipulated in *The National Education Guidelines.* Monitored practice reduces the vision/reality gap by promoting learning and change of practice resulting from:
- Assessment systems that aim to produce quality evidence;
- Analysis of evidence by which to judge progress in line with vision;
- Use of base line data for strategic planning usage;
- Renewal of practice and systems in response to need; and
- Consistency of systems, processes and structures in practice.

Monitored practice is, in itself, a layered activity. On a mandatory level, appraisals, self-reviews, reporting to the board and the Ministry of Education on progress and achievement ensures accountability but in the form of *compliance.* On an informal level, monitored practice that involves peer reviews, self-reviews, professional dialogue and informal feedback ensures accountability but in the form of *professional commitment* to self, colleagues, students and parents. Both have the potential to build capacity in ways previously indicated.

PROFESSIONAL DEVELOPMENT: CAPACITY BUILDING LINKS

In this school, professional development is regarded as change inducing resulting from:

- Keeping up to date with current trends: *We are more up with new initiatives that are happening. In the past it's been we can't be doing this – now it's a lot on the go. A lot more things to keep people motivated and enthused;*
- Doing the job better: *Teachers' own knowledge and their own professional development have been lifted. This has impacted on the learning. You're not plucking things so much out of the air and you can focus on the teaching and the learning;*
- Tracking benefits of learning to students: *Like with myself, I wasn't into it at all and at times I would avoid it and that was to the detriment of the children. Now that I have gone on the numeracy project you know what you are doing. It's awesome to be involved and this flows on to the kids;* and
- Enhancing personal growth: *Improving constantly and knowing more about what they are doing ... focused on the students and where they actually need to go and what they are working towards.*

One of the concerns related to building capacity for school improvement is sustainment of professional learning; that is, sustaining the impetus for change following initiation and implementation of new innovations. This school's responses to sustainment include:

- Professional development that maintains a 'working towards vision' attitude;
- Layering of professional development that addresses school and stakeholder needs;
- Balanced attention to developing individual, collective and/or systemic capacities;
- Buy-in to practices of collaborative interchange, reflective practice and openness to new ideas;
- Management of professional development that involves flexibility, relevance and scaffolded learning;
- Inclusion of parents in the education milieu; and
- Building a community of learners focused on student centered learning, empowerment, improvement and community.

CONCLUSION

Professional development in this school sits at the internal/external interface (see Figure 5.2). From this position, as signalled earlier, it has positive implications for all school stakeholders. For students, this translates to meeting individual needs, increased motivation to learn, improved levels of academic attainment, self-efficacy and enhanced teacher-student relationships. For staff it means *working with what you have got and trying to make it better* and sustaining learning that is student centred, improvement orientated, empowering and builds community. Externally and internally sourced professional development creates an eclectic knowledge base useful in guiding decision-making. Trust, risk taking and motivation to change are promoted and supported. For parents, professional development means: increased educational and personal knowledge to assist in their children's education, preparedness to become more involved in school life, heightened awareness and understanding of other cultures and, for some, a deeper awareness of the New Zealand way of life. Systemic benefits include: altered practice in response to new information, systemic coherence, closure of the vision/reality gap, and bridging and buffering safeguards that manage conflicting tensions. Professional development assists with change management in sustainment of capacity building for school improvement.

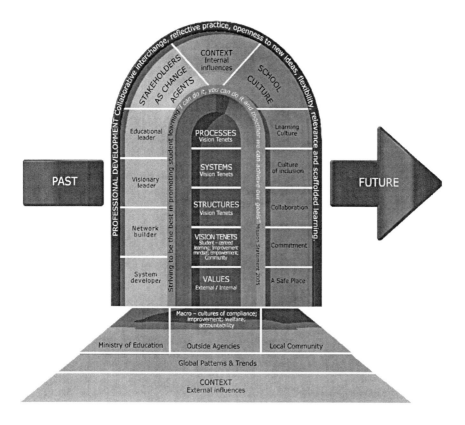

Figure 5.2 School Attribute: Professional Development

NOTES

[xviii] 'Outside agencies' is a generic label used to cover representatives from various groups who provide professional input. Data collected identified the following as having had or in the year of data collection were observed as influencing this school's professional development. These include: RTLB; GSE; Team Solutions; Project Early Staff; Ministry of Education contract facilitators (ICT and Numeracy project); and the facilitator for Music.

[xix] Te Kete Ipurangi (TKI) is a website giving teachers and principals access to teaching, education information, and communication with colleagues.

[xx] Purposeful learning or purpose driven learning is defined as meeting the needs of stakeholders in line with vision tenets.

[xxi] The aims of the Numeracy Professional Development Projects are to improve student achievement in mathematics by improving classroom teaching at all levels. The projects improve teacher confidence through addressing content knowledge and understanding of effective teaching and learning in Mathematics. Projects undertaken by this school include the Early Numeracy Project (ENP) for years 0-3 and Advanced Numeracy Project (ANP) for years 4-6.

[xxii] The first ICT Strategy for Schools was released in 1998. The goals of this strategy were to build infrastructure and school capability. Digital Horizons was released in June 2002. This strategy focuses on integrating ICT more fully into curriculum practice.

[xxiii] The Parent Mentoring Initiative was funded by the Ministry of Education between 2002-2005. The aims were to strengthen relationship through a bi-directional partnership between parents/caregivers and teachers; parents and children and families/communities and schools in order to support the educational achievement of learners. The initiative sought also to establish mutual responsibility and accountability around these partnerships.

[xxiv] Introductory Professional Development Programme for Teacher Aides/Kaiawhina in literacy development.

[xxv] Team work was witnessed in: whole school staff and team meetings; literacy curriculum meetings; senior management meetings; parent/school meetings such as board and Friends of the School; and in school events such as assemblies and other celebratory type events.

[xxvi] Team work as part of school organisation means the school is divided into three syndicates: junior, middle and senior. In addition, staff meet and engage in other forms of team work – coordination of: curriculum, special needs/abilities and cultural groups; senior management and teacher aides meetings.

SCHOOL PRACTICE

Knowledge Production and Utilisation

Contemporary literature appears profuse in descriptive studies focused on particular school improvement programmes and projects (Harris, 2003) emphasising: professional development (Fullan & Mascall, 2000); mandated reform policies, targeted outcomes and tightened lines of accountabilities (Leithwood, 2001); leadership models for example, moral (Sergiovanni, 2006), visionary (Sammons, Thomas & Mortimer, 1997), managerial (Slee, Weiner, & Tomlinson, 1998), and transformational (Leithwood & Jantzi, 1999); vision (Fullan, 1993); and school culture (Stoll, 1999). As is the case in New Zealand and other countries, compliance and accountability agendas at the macro political level account for the many systems, processes and structures aimed at measuring and reporting on improvement to student outcomes. Teacher appraisals, curriculum reviews and internal and external school audits are some examples of measures regarded necessary when it comes to tracking and reporting on improvement. However, such mechanisms fail to capture holistically the notion of what happens in practice in terms of capacity building for improvement to raise student outcomes.

Chapters 2 to 5 described vision, stakeholders as change agents, school culture and professional development as attributes of capacity building for improvement. However, attributes in themselves are insufficient in explaining processes which necessitates a deeper examination of practice.

Chapter 6 and the two which follow hone in on capacity building practices namely: knowledge production and utilisation; a switching on mentality; and division of labour: roles and responsibilities. In Chapters 6, 7 and 8, attributes are reviewed in terms of fostering practices. Figure 6.1 captures the notion of practices informing capacity building for improvement. Practices are positioned above vision and encapsulated by the other attributes. To illustrate how each practice contributes to capacity building for school improvement, vignettes from practice are inserted.

A central concern for schools in pursuit of improvement is their capacity to initiate, manage and sustain improvement based on reliable, authentic information. Yet, in this regard, a paucity of research exists (Hadfield, Chapman, Curryer, & Barrett, 2004). Chapter 6 commences this discussion on practices by focussing attention on knowledge production and utilisation. It highlights key aspects of this practice namely; collaborative interchange of information, reflective practice, stakeholder networking and systemic development. The chapter ends with

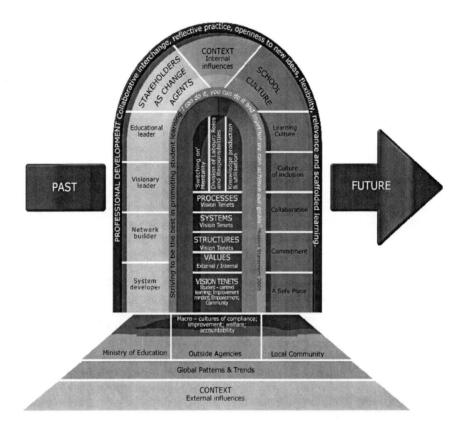

Figure 6.1 School Practices: Knowledge Production and Utilisation; Switching on Mentality; Division of Labour: Roles and Responsibilities

concluding statements of how the practice of knowledge production and utilisation contributes to capacity building for school improvement.

CONTRIBUTION OF ATTRIBUTES TO KNOWLEDGE PRODUCTION AND UTILISATION

At the core of all capacity building for school improvement activity is vision captured as 'striving to be the best in promoting student learning'. Four tenets in support of the vision are: student centered learning, improvement mindset, empowerment and community. The mission statement, *I can do it, you can do it and together we can achieve our goals* fuels the passion necessary to reduce the vision/practice gap. The school's vision is not only articulated but, also, documented in strategic plans making it a blueprint or map that guides practice. School stakeholders' involvement in vision conceptualisation, transmission, and evolution aligns with external and internal change demands. The school's vision, underpinned by macro and micro value sets, serves as a bridge connecting the school with its environment. Such connecting links work in the best interest of the school and its stakeholders as all activities prioritise student outcomes, improvement, empowerment and community. Placed at the forefront of all activity, the vision drives knowledge production and utilisation in promoting learning.

Capacity building for school improvement is concerned with change and management of change. All change disestablishes equilibrium and increases uncertainty as new ways of doing things are required. The attribute of school stakeholders as change agents is important in the knowledge production and utilisation process because, as change agents, stakeholders encourage inquiry into 'how things are done'. The raising of doubt, a product of inquiry, is considered appropriate when seeking opinion, scrutinising and analysing data and taking action to improve it. In this school, modification of teaching practice and motivation to pursue and support change from within is a collective enterprise accomplished by all stakeholders. Regular conversations help create knowledge from new information to:

- Give meaning to the work people do in this school;
- Generate shared values, beliefs and norms that value learning;
- Promote sense in the knowledge production and utilisation process;
- Facilitate socially shared and transmitted knowledge in meeting needs;
- Ensure consistency of action;
- Create a professional learning community identity; and
- Enhance a working towards vision stance.

Deal and Kennedy (1982) define culture as 'the way we do things around here'. Beare, Caldwell and Millikan (1989) refer to culture as verbal, behavioural and visual manifestations enacted in practice. Schein (1985) defines the concept as, "basic assumptions and beliefs that are shared by members of an organisation, that operate unconsciously, and that define in a basic 'taken-for-granted' fashion an organisation's view of itself and its environment" (p. 6).

In this school, the vision sustains a culture that values learning, inclusivity, collaboration, commitment, community and safety. Attention is given to social cohesion and work place arrangements which enhance collaboration and professionalism. All stakeholders connect with and value learning. Valuing learning means engineering time and place for collective dialogue or learning talk to occur. Valuing learning generates a professional learning community ethos inclusive of all. In an environment that pushes for reform, a collaborative culture appears promising in building capacity for improvement because it minimises problems of individualism, balkanisation and contrived collegiality.

The value of collaborative cultures linked to school improvement is endorsed by many authors (see for example Nias et al.'s study). In Nias et al.'s study (1989), a culture of collaboration was seen to embody a set of societal and moral beliefs about desirable relationships between individuals and communities and not from beliefs about epistemology or pedagogy. Two main points that emerged from this study were that individuals should be accepted and valued and so too should the interdependence that exists between groups and teams. Interdependence, the authors note, leads to "mutual constraint and it is the resulting security which encourages members of the culture to be open with one another in the expression of disagreement and of emotion" (p. 74). Shared understandings and agreed behaviours amongst members of a group enable trust and learning from each other to flourish. Nias et al. comment, "the relationships which they create in the process are tough and flexible enough to withstand shocks and uncertainties from within and without" (p. 74).

This school's culture of collaboration fosters team work and community spirit. School systems, structures and processes support collaboration. They offer channels and opportunities for collective dialogue and collaborative decision-making. In the spirit of collaboration, knowledge is produced at various levels through mutual dependence and professional interdependencies. Commitment to doing what's best for the school and its stakeholders builds trust in people to act professionally both as individuals and within a collective. Group ways of working account for distributed practice (Gronn, 2002), mutual trust (Codd, 2005), empowerment and networks of support (Muijs & Harris, 2003) to ensure that optimal social cohesion and control and high expectations support and advance the practice of knowledge production and utilisation.

Literature suggests professional development raises teacher professionalism (MOE, 1999a) and initiates school improvement (see for example, Barth, 1990; Fullan & Mascall, 2000; Alton-Lee, 2003). In this school, learning is a result of collaboration that encourages teachers to work and talk to one another on issues of improving practice. Collaborative professional development is linked with the social processing of knowledge to enhance learning. It is focused on tangible outcomes as stated in reviews and strategic plans. It facilitates access to new information to meet individual, collective and systemic need.

Professional development on offer in this school is best described as a situated, layered approach to learning with connections built in at the individual, collective and systemic levels of practice. The preferred way of working in this school is in teams. For this to happen, new ideas introduced at a collective level are developed in teams and amongst individuals in an attempt to establish meaning and purpose. The learning that eventuates is specific to context. A layered approach to learning is a product of shared responsibility that creates connectedness through conversations around teaching and learning. Knowledge production and utilisation that results enhances systemic coherence, consistency of practice and a learning enriched environment (Rosenholtz, 1989) encouraging learning on a daily basis.

ASPECTS OF KNOWLEDGE PRODUCTION AND UTILISATION

There are several aspects of the knowledge production and utilisation practice that adds to generating capacity for school improvement. In this section, vignettes accompany explanations to highlight collaborative interchange of information, reflective practice, stakeholder networking, and systemic development.

The first aspect relates to collaborative interchange of information. Observations at staff, team and curriculum meetings confirm that staff collaboration in the exchange of information is embedded in the school's culture and forms part of daily activity. Collaborative interchange of information expands on mere compliance or development of collegial relationships and facilitates, instead, the asking of 'hard' questions of existing practice in the form of what is beneficial and, likewise, of impediment in the learning/goal achievement process. Collective working through of issues encourages reflection on practice in an effort to build individual, collective and systemic learning capacities. It is the social processing of knowledge among stakeholders that facilitates learning and refinement of systems, processes and structures in support of improvement. The following vignette illustrates collaborative interchange in constructing an integrated teaching unit.

> The session was facilitated by the deputy principal who invited staff to contribute resources and ideas towards planning a unit of work. Knowledge sharing is one way of avoiding information hoarding that can occur among teams. Creation of a combined knowledge pool through sharing ideas was followed by guidance on how to plan an integrated unit. Opportunities for teachers to utilise available information in the generation of year level plans were provided. During this activity, year level teams of teachers were engaged in deconstructing curriculum documents, reinforcing planning requirements as stipulated in school policy and locating and distributing information on the topic. This activity lasted an hour followed by feedback on learning outcomes, experiences and methods of assessment.

This vignette highlights the importance of collaborative interchange of information that goes further than task accomplishment. Talking through issues of teaching and learning reinforces and extends existing knowledge bases within a collective. Learning conversations facilitate individual and collective advancement of knowledge, school-wide systemic cohesiveness and consistency of practice. Feedback establishes common understandings of learning outcomes, experiences and assessment across age levels. It cements in all teachers' minds what to expect from students in terms of abilities and skills at various ages and stages of development. Collaborative interchange of information contributes to:
– Shared involvement in task accomplishment;
– Opportunities to modify and adapt the curriculum and system in line with the needs of students;
– Opportunities to promote a collaborative learning culture; and
– Construction of systems, processes and procedures to facilitate consistency of practice.
Another aspect of knowledge production and utilisation is reflective practice. Reflective practice is linked to the school's vision. Here, the attention is on assessment and evaluation of data collected through reviews which identify need. Reflective practice can be individual, in the form of teacher appraisals or peer reviews where teaching staff consider and evaluate their practice as a group. Reflection always involves an analysis of data to improve practice and student

outcomes. Reflective practice has the potential to stimulate new ways of doing things because it is accompanied by a search for answers to 'Why?' and 'With what effect?' questions. Reflection creates positive interdependencies among stakeholders to advance:

– Rigorous analysis of data in identification and assessment of school/stakeholder need;
– Empowerment of staff in the knowledge production and utilisation process;
– Continuous professional input and 'openness to new ideas' for individual and collective learning;
– Problem solving within self-governing/self-managing frameworks; and
– Development of creative and flexible systems, processes and structures in response to need.

The vignette chosen to highlight reflective practice is one where teachers were encouraged to reflect on current literacy strategies aimed at increasing ESOL[xxvii] students' oral language capabilities. Two staff members with literacy expertise facilitated the session.

> The first facilitator asked: 'Are we doing the best for our ESOL children? Is the child hearing what you are saying? How do you know? How do we support our ESOL children in their vocabulary development?' She initiated discussion by providing ESOL literacy test results. Teachers were guided in their examination of students' oral language scripts. Group feedback engendered debate: 'they (students) don't have much vocabulary; all these 'negatives' – this is a worry; but a 'no would be because they were reluctant to talk'. The facilitator guided discussion to, 'so what does this all mean for teaching?' Ideas discussed indicated consideration of alternative instruction to enhance oral language development.

> The second facilitator shared information on 'three level guides', a strategy with potential to assist students' processing of information to higher levels. This part of the session commenced with ascertaining teachers' prior knowledge on strategy use. The message continually reinforced was, 'You are trying to push for deeper levels of thinking'.

Processes of reflective practice, albeit individual, collective and/or systemic, are documented and these documents form the basis for further reviews, modification of practice, systemic change, vision enhancement and individual and collective learning.

Knowledge production and utilisation is a product of stakeholder networking. Networking implies association or connection with others in the knowledge production and utilisation process. Internally facilitated networks generate situated knowledge. New knowledge brought into the school by course attendance, outside agency support and buy-in to Ministry of Education contracts expands the existing pool of site-based knowledge. Externally sourced information, shared with others, engenders new insights on practice. Sharing ideas in collaborative ways develops awareness of one's own ability to influence the learning of others. Everyone is considered a leader in the knowledge production and utilisation process. In this next vignette, a teacher with technology curriculum responsibility ran a staff meeting on information gained at a course she had attended.

> The staff member handed out technology exemplars and invited teachers to examine the material in pairs. She handed out a matrix with grade level technology indicators. An explanation of each was provided and teachers asked to consider their students' progression across the levels. Teachers were encouraged to use the matrix to note year level learning outcomes. By way of feedback, comments received focused on ways to improve practice. The teacher pushed for systemic change by asking, 'Where do you think we should go next and what should be our next learning target?'

From this vignette, the following points emerge as important: synthesis of old and new knowledge to achieve fresh levels of understanding; future goal setting and pedagogical improvement; and the need for systemic support to create and support change. Social norms of collaboration and a team ethos meant that all were involved in the development of a collective body of information. This promotes an expansive knowledge base which advances individual, collective and systemic knowledge capacities.

The last aspect of knowledge production and utilisation is linked to systemic development. This extends beyond consideration of individual and collective learning to renewal of systems, processes and structures in light of changing conditions. One way of achieving this is through on-going curriculum and school reviews as captured in Figure 5.1. Reviews identify strengths and weaknesses of programmes and practices linked to student and school improvement. Reviews develop an authentic base for decision-making which promotes:

- Reflection that is individual, collective, systemic and future orientated;
- Increased knowledge on school practices, curriculum, pedagogy and stakeholder/system needs;
- Growth and development of a learning culture;
- Opportunities to adapt and modify practice in response to changing conditions;
- Knowledge production and utilisation in pursuit of vision ideals; and
- System coherence and consistency of practice.

CONCLUSION: LINKS TO CAPACITY BUILDING FOR SCHOOL IMPROVEMENT

School improvement is very much concerned with developing teacher pedagogical practice related to student learning. Such a perspective reinforces an improvement mindset, empowerment and a learning community ethos. Collaborative interchange of information, reflection, networking and systemic development strengthen the social processing of information to create and extend individual, collective and systemic knowledge. Aforementioned aspects establish group learning norms that sustain and reinforce continuous cycles of knowledge production and utilisation to build capacity for school improvement.

Practices of knowledge production and utilisation enhance connectedness amongst stakeholders in learning. They create a professional learning culture where everyone is considered a learner, a leader, a catalyst for change and a change agent. Opportunities for professional development promote lifelong learning mindsets. Mutual respect and trust that emerge facilitate the raising of doubt and the asking of 'hard questions' to alter habits and beliefs in the betterment of teaching and learning. Collective dialogue and reflection generates knowledge at the individual, collective and systemic levels of practice. Monitoring of practice ensures learning happens to benefit students. Knowledge production and utilisation strategies mean attention is always focused on achieving the vision ideal, 'striving to be the best in promoting student learning'.

NOTES

[xxvii] ESOL – English Speakers of Other Languages.

SCHOOL PRACTICE

'Switching on' Mentality

No matter where you teach there are social pressures, student related issues plus an array of institutional regulations and constraints that need attention over and above the school improvement and capacity building agenda. Despite this, school principals, senior managers, boards of trustees, teachers and parents pursue pathways that lead to capacity building for school improvement. A school is one of the few workplace environments where people who have a say in what happens can experience commitment and creativity towards directing and leading change. But, how is this fostered? How do we sustain the drive for school improvement given the numerous challenges of context? What happens *in situ* that energises people and engages them to exercise long term passion for improvement? What systems, processes and structures enlist collaborative endeavours to respond to the somewhat rapid pace of change in meeting individual, collective and systemic need? The answer to these and other questions focus on the very heart of school life – its 'culture'. If how a school builds its capacity for school improvement is a product of the ways people think, interact and act, then, questions need to be asked on what fosters the quality of thinking, interacting and acting in line with building capacity for improvement?

In the case study school, the culture created contained the following hallmarks: collaboration, a learning culture, a culture of inclusion, commitment and a 'safe' place. It was defined as: *where everybody gets involved like the staff, the families and everything. We all want to be a part of it.* Such a culture creates a 'switching on' mentality where the interpersonal mode of practice encourages commitment, passion and energy in the building of capacity for improvement. In Chapter 7, observations of school practice detail the 'emotional' and practical actions of stakeholders to define what I call a 'switching on' mentality. I start by recapping on how the four attributes contribute to the emergence of this practice and, as with the previous chapter, provide vignettes to illustrate the nature of this practice in context.

'SWITCHING ON' MENTALITY THROUGH VISION

Vision generates connectedness among stakeholders to a common purpose which, in this school, is 'striving to be the best in promoting student learning'. Connectedness to vision accounts for the following descriptors: *It's really positive and encouraging; I feel proud to be part of that to be honest;* and *You know the people out in the wider community look at our school and know it is a good place to send their kids and that they are going to get a really good deal.* The vision, embedded in the culture, enhances deeper inquiry into practice in response to: *Where do we want to be?* Stakeholders' responses to the *where do we want to be* question essentially sustains the drive needed to build capacity for improvement. It creates opportunities to steer a pathway towards improvement. The adjustment and modification to vision undertaken by various stakeholders creates a sense of ownership and buy-in to a common cause. The process is energising. The following vignette captures stakeholders debating the *where do we want to be* question in the construction of a new mission statement so as to better address the vision/practice application:

> At a board meeting, the principal asked, 'Are you happy with the mission statement or can it be changed? We want something that people can espouse'. Much discussion was invoked on the existing mission statement: 'we want to put in the word positive before learning'; 'Perhaps we need to say develop organisation skills which include goal setting. It comes back to the values. Perhaps we need to say: To enable the students to give and receive feedback'. At this stage, the conversation was mainly teacher generated. One board member noted, 'The 'You Can Do It' programme is taught but doesn't the 'You Can Do It' underpin the school?' This generated the following conversation:
>
> Principal: 'It started as a programme but is beginning to be a mantra underpinning the school'.
>
> Senior teacher 1: 'Shall it be part of the mission statement?'
>
> Deputy Principal: 'Might not be part of the mission statement for ever. We could be using another programme. The programme is a tool. Still we need to mention it'.
>
> Principal: 'The 'You Can Do It' is filtering through though'.
>
> Board member 1: 'I think it should be in the mission statement'.
>
> Board member 2: 'This is emphasised in all newsletters'.
>
> Senior teacher 2: 'Maybe we should leave the 'You Can Do It' in the values section'.
>
> Principal: 'I would like a short snappy mission statement. I think it is part of the school too'.
>
> Board member 1: 'It is part of the discipline programme too'.

Principal: 'If I came to this school as a visitor I would get nothing from the mission statement. What about a 'You Can Do It' community'.

Deputy Principal: 'Why don't we say I can do it learning community?'

Senior teacher 3: 'Yes that's what we want'.

Assistant Principal: 'You can do it means that there is someone else supporting you'.

Deputy Principal: 'I would be happy with that'.

Principal: 'What about 'I can do it. You can do it?'

Senior teacher 2: 'Yes that gets the belief out to the community'.

Board member 2: 'That brings the people on board'.

Senior teacher 2: 'I like the word together'.

Deputy Principal: 'I can do it, you can do it and together we can achieve our goals'.

This conversation produced the new mission statement: *I can do it, you can do it and together we can achieve our goals*; a statement born from collaborative interchange, reflection and inclusion of various viewpoints to represent this school's identity.

Several principles emerge from this vignette that explains how processes in this school lead to a 'switching on' mentality. To begin, collaboration among stakeholders encourages a sharing of views. Collaborative interchange, reflection and valuing what others have to say create openness to new ideas and flexibility. Alongside this, a strong desire to negotiate win-win outcomes emerges not only as seen in the example but, also, across the school at different sites. When opportunities arise for dialogue on practice, issues are raised and debated and in doing this, adjustments made to viewpoints reflect a binding concern for others and adherence to a vision that draws people together. This leads to optimism and support for the four tenets of student centred learning, an improvement mindset, empowerment and community.

'SWITCHING ON' MENTALITY THROUGH CULTURE

Calls to collaborate are openly voiced, described as *the arrows go everywhere*. A logical end point to cementing the need to collaborate is a consideration of how this school can build its capacity to improve. The practices of stakeholders are organised around a number of core values such as respect, fairness, equality, honesty, safety, acceptance and community. It is clear that this practice is dedicated to the welfare of staff, students and parents rather than being purely instrumental in serving economic reasons or solely compliance driven. Alongside these qualities are examples of stakeholders being firm in relation to expectations and standards and, on occasions, taking a tough stand in applying pressure while seeking fairness. In the following vignette, the call to collaborate was observed as enforcement of democratic ways of working. The vignette presented demonstrates an attempt to engender collective responsibility for staff representation at monthly 'Friends of the School' meetings.

> A staff member noted that representation on a regular basis by one staff member at the 'Friends of the School' meetings needed reconsideration. In her words, "Going out to this meeting and attending another meeting is just too much for one person in one week". The staff member suggested that staff representation at 'Friends of the School' meetings should demonstrate collective responsibility. The request was duly noted and senior staff made aware of calls to restructure this role. This request was discussed at both senior team and staff levels with agreement reached that all staff should share in the responsibility of representing the school at 'Friends of the School' meetings.

The vignette reveals that a culture of collaboration is not something solely concerned with the development of a learning culture or linked to displays of shared roles and responsibilities. Collaboration is a cultural hallmark valued in sustaining democratic ways of working. It forms part of the social glue that binds this group together. In the vignette provided, senior staff acted ethically by not dismissing calls to alter practice. They opened the situation up for debate that initiated changes. Responding to such challenges in ethical ways dictates how things are around here. Empowerment that ensues means *teachers feel that they have a say in what is happening. So it's not something that's been put down from above but that the teachers have some ownership of it as well.*

Collaboration is willingness to help without being asked and having an expectation that support is available should the need arise. Language that captures this is collective use of 'we'. Underpinning frequent use of 'we' are values of respect, collegiality, fun, tolerance and community as this vignette indicates:

> The event observed occurred at a syndicate meeting where team members jointly constructed a farewell programme for a teacher leaving the school. The senior teacher stated, "We need to fix up the assembly roster for this special occasion. Who would like to get the speakers?" Teachers willingly opted to fulfill task requirements such as: collecting letters of thanks from children, arranging musical items, putting on a play and buying an appropriate gift of thanks.

The whole notion of 'safe' place is highlighted in this school. This is partly to avoid repeating unsafe dysfunctional habits of the past and more importantly, move forward in an environment where feeling safe and trust are valued. Trust in people, processes and systems create environments where freedom to question and raise debate flourishes. The synergy this creates raises commitment and energy and makes task completion enjoyable, manageable and ethical as illustrated in the following vignette:

> Planning an integrated science/technology unit involved all team members working collaboratively. The senior teacher handed out a unit plan and encouraged team members to adapt it for collective use, "Let's do some brainstorming of our own of all the ideas to do with healthy construction of ice blocks". Collaboration denotes professional trust in members to contribute tacit knowledge for collective group benefit. Decision-making reinforces professional and personal trust among individuals to work for the benefit of others. An atmosphere of trust facilitates critique of practice in an effort to improve it. In this school, collaboration, teamness, doing one's best, respect for the others, learning and improvement are placed at the forefront of all activity. All facets of team work elevate individual and collective well-being as important.

'SWITCHING ON' MENTALITY THROUGH PROFESSIONAL LEARNING

If we are to engage in capacity building for school improvement then we need to view the school as a learning system where collaborative interaction among stakeholders creates dialogue which enhances the social and intellectual capital of the individual, collective and the system. The role of stakeholders as agents of change in learning is powerful because it opens up the possibility of creativity. To create a 'switching on' mentality through professional learning is not an easy option. It requires reflection and value debates on work to establish meaning and relevance. Reflection and value debates in this school operate at a deeper level of practice where attention on 'purpose' and justification for action generates the asking of hard questions towards a 'working with vision' stance. In doing so, stakeholders' voice opinions, engage with others to achieve reciprocal understanding and provide explanations, observations and modeling of new ways of doing things to stimulate insights and possibilities for improvement. Such actions promote a 'switching on' mentality by taking seriously the voices and actions of others. Each individual, operating from a position of self as a contributor to the collective and the system, creates a groundswell of passion and support for capacity building and school improvement. A 'switching on' mentality through professional learning offers:
- A readiness for change;
- Receptivity and preparedness to make adjustments and modification in response to internal and external shifting dynamics; and
- Insistence on collective input in processes of decision-making.

In this school, professional learning assumes a layered approach. Whole staff professional development meetings occur weekly. Having begun conversations on practice at such meetings, teaching staff take the ideas to the team level for discussion. This is where modified learning in year level teams takes place. Ideas are also discussed at the curriculum team meetings. School structural arrangements create the potential for discussion across levels and amongst staff. Membership in the curriculum teams remains open to those with a particular interest. Ideas discussed within teams are brought back to the whole school forum which encourages further modification according to 'fit'. When new ideas are mulled around in this way, there is always an applicability element attached which makes the discussion fruitful. This has the potential to produce critical thought in regard to what is necessary to build capacity for improvement. This school's structural arrangements promote professional learning in a safe, collaborative, committed environment. Talk that focuses on real world experiences are stimulating for those involved. Throughout this process it is possible to see teams of learners as well as individuals engage in reiterative cycles of processing new information to be applied in context. The school's structural arrangements create a systemic way of moving forward albeit personally, collectively and systemically. The process of reciprocal meaning making is a powerful motivator to 'switch on' and maintain a drive to learn and contribute to the building of capacity for improvement.

'SWITCHING ON' MENTALITY THROUGH COMMUNITY

Stakeholders in this school are involved in many networks. Networking is focused on working in a culture defined as community. Teachers maintain that parental involvement builds community ethos. Parents demonstrate loyalty to the school and staff by managing school resources, helping out at special events, assisting with in class support, leading cultural group activities and raising funds. It is safe to say that parental input helps raise the human, social and fiscal capacities of this school.
'Staff patterns of behaviour also support this notion of community. Shared roles and responsibilities promote a giving and sharing attitude in the service of others. The feeling of togetherness is empowering and necessary to support the work of stakeholders. In this school 'switching on' is connected to being a community.

'SWITCHING ON' MENTALITY THROUGH SYSTEMS, PROCESSES AND STRUCTURES

Systems, processes and structures foster a 'switching on' mentality. Stakeholders note that systems, processes and structures *make them feel that they are valued as they provide for ease, creativity and flexibility and all those things*. Systems, processes and structures allow for:
- Pastoral caring that makes people feel that they can do things;
- Flexibility to meet situational demands;
- Change that is managed, supported and monitored;
- Support – the leaders are always there; and
- Closure of the vision/reality gap.

− An example of a school structure (inclusive of inherent systems and processes) that promotes this 'switching on' mentality is the school assembly. At school assemblies, rituals and behaviour patterns reinforce this school as a fun, rewarding place of learning. Assemblies are structures where:
− The vision ideal is reinforced and transmitted;
− Vision tenets are enforced;
− Work undertaken is acknowledged; and
− Achievements are celebrated.

Assemblies are positively charged school events. Awards are given to students on a regular basis. These include: golden box award,[xxviii] certificates for academic and other achievements, spot prizes for participation and rewards for supporting wider school events such as the 'Fun Fiesta night'.

Assemblies are action orientated events with built-in opportunities for fun. For example, at one assembly, a teacher aide dressed up in a multi coloured outfit because of a dare[xxix] she had with the principal. The story of the dare was recounted and shared to the audience's amusement. Jump-jam activities at assemblies are regular energising events that encourage collective participation. Parents join in with jump-jam and other activities. Parents bring along their pre-schoolers creating a family atmosphere. The message promoted is that this is a community school. Messages enforced at assemblies support the vision. Student centred learning is awarded attention with improvement high on the agenda. School assemblies promote the message that this school is a safe place with a positive, 'switched on' mentality promoting learning.

CONCLUSION: LINKS TO CAPACITY BUILDING FOR SCHOOL IMPROVEMENT

Switching on mentality endorses collaboration and collegiality. This school is seen as a place with a *heart* that beats strong. It is a place where people want to be because:

− People feel they are listened to, their voices are heard. The atmosphere builds trusting relationships as *you are allowed to say what you want to say or say how you feel and they're not going to shout you down*;
− The stance adopted is action orientated with openness to new ideas as this comment implies: *We were talking about the old hall and saying it is really small. So it took some time. They were planning it for twelve years. But it is happening now*;
− Collaboration is endorsed, *the thing is all the leaders, the team leaders what they do is they try to ask other teachers their opinion for example about books that they need to buy*;
− Open, transparent communication is practised. For example, *when things are happening they do tell us and so all of us know the same thing*; and
− Integrity is valued, *I have found that the (principal) and (deputy principal) take things on board...so its lots of practice before they say things and they do it and they show us and they say see this is how it can be done.*

NOTES

[xxviii] Teachers on playground duty reward children caught doing the right thing in terms of behaviour. The children's names are put into the box and students whose names are drawn out at assemblies receive small tangible rewards. Certificates are awarded for academic and non-academic achievement.

[xxix] The dare concerned the building of the new school hall. The school had been planning to build a new hall for the last twelve years. Most staff members were resigned to this not eventuating for some time. The teacher aide happened to mention this to the principal who confirmed the building would commence by the end of the month.

CHAPTER 8

SCHOOL PRACTICE: DIVISION OF LABOUR

Roles and Responsibilities

Connell (1985) states: "Teachers are workers, teaching is work, and the school is a workplace" (p. 69). In this era of reform and burgeoning responsibilities, the concept of a situated 'workplace' is popular but needs defining as from this starting point, roles and responsibilities of stakeholders with a focus on capacity building for school improvement can be made. Chapter 5 examined the actions and contributions of the principal, board of trustees, senior staff, teachers and parents as change agents. In Chapter 8, roles and responsibilities of stakeholders within a division of labour paradigm are explored in relation to school practice and links to capacity building for improvement.

WORKPLACE NETWORKING

The workplace is an enmeshed ecosystem connected to the external/internal environment. It is reflective of the structures in the school itself. In the case study school, designated structures and stakeholders' roles and responsibilities within them create a working community ethos. Stakeholders' roles and responsibilities are delineated reflective of their position in the school. For example, at the governance level, board of trustees and staff work collaboratively to ensure the school meets *The National Education Guidelines* and reports to the Ministry on its stated aims and objectives. Board members have designated roles and responsibilities associated with curriculum, finance, property and personnel portfolios. The principal reports on curriculum, staffing and other issues. The staff representative represents the views of the staff to the board.

At the school level of functioning, designated teaching and administrative roles and responsibilities of staff represent another form of workplace networking. The principal manages the day to day operation of the school. Deputy and assistant principals are middle managers with administrative and teaching responsibilities. Senior teachers manage syndicates and undertake curriculum and systemic delegated tasks. Specialist staff members have assigned job descriptions. For example, the Special Education Needs Coordinator (SENCO), English Speakers of Other Languages (ESOL) coordinator and reading recovery teachers establish and maintain systems that meet specific student, staff and systemic needs. Teachers have roles and responsibilities for classroom management and, in some cases, workplace development related to curriculum responsibilities.

Another layer of workplace networking involves support staff (teacher aides, bi-lingual support workers, secretaries, school caretaker and ground personnel) fulfilling their delegated work responsibilities. Their work patterns are flexible to 'fit' workplace demands. Although there is a fixed element to their schedules, flexibility and negotiation are continually called for with respect to site-based conditions which alter in response to students' needs. This may occur during the term, on completion of work, or even daily.

Although each staff member is aware of the others' work related roles and responsibilities, patterns of behaviour suggest that demarcated roles and responsibilities appear enmeshed, more in keeping with the social norms of collaboration that require a giving of self for the benefit of others. Reflective of this school's culture, the workplace as a community is where people contribute to the well-being of others. Having said this, however, constant demands for change in response to external and internal requirements mean ongoing adjustment to existing roles and responsibilities. External demands impose *extra work* in accommodating curriculum changes and meeting compliance within national directives. Internal demands (such as, sudden staff departure) necessitate adaptation and modification of roles and responsibilities to suit altered conditions. Renegotiation and modification of roles and responsibilities demands a 'working with change' attitude to maintain systemic equilibrium and minimise resistance to change. In this self-managing school context, working with change adopts a division of labour: roles and responsibilities focus and a '*working as a team*' ethos. Team work enhances collaboration, reflective practice, networking and systemic development.

THE ROLE OF VISION

As signalled in earlier chapters, the school's vision provides a unified sense of direction captured as, 'striving to be the best in promoting student learning'. *I can do it, you can do it and together we can achieve our goals* mission statement and the four support tenets are endorsed verbally, in documentation and through stakeholder' actions. Vision construction involves processes of conceptualisation, transmission and evolution. The processes are symbolic of the recognition given to stakeholder voice to ensure 'fit' with context. Staff and parents collective input ensures the vision builds on past experiences, is future orientated and embedded in current practice. Vision conceptualisation and steps taken towards transmission and evolution necessitate:

- Teamness, a sharing of views with others to promote agreed goals for future action;
- Accountability of goal achievement where progress is 'ticked off' and next steps added;
- Room for individual, collective and systemic growth;
- Transparency of past and current achievements combined with future goals; and
- Compliance to Ministry of Education demands that renders this school a 'safe place'.

In this setting, all school stakeholders assume roles of vision guardianship. In practice, this equates to: challenging existing practice, empowering others to bring about change, providing systemic support and reviewing and adjusting strategies to achieve improvement. The vignette presented below illustrates a teacher's allegiance to implementing vision tenets in an attempt to improve practice:

> The teacher had attended a weekend course on gifted and talented students. On return, she reported on new learning gained. She reminded staff that although this school is not located in a high socio-economic area, it has students who display exceptional skills and abilities. She introduced a gifted and talented identification guide from the course and requested staff discuss its strengths and limitations. She identified school personnel who could assist in identification of students with exceptional abilities. Policy change, she noted, was a necessary part of accommodating new procedures, practices and legislative mandates. She informed staff that the director of the 'Gifted and Talented' association had been invited to run further professional development sessions on the topic. This was in response to interest and the need for further action expressed by staff members.

Vision guardianship is orchestrated to form a part of everyone's roles and responsibilities. As captured in the vignette, implementing vision ideals in practice is aimed at:
– Exercising vigilance in identifying students' needs;
– Seeking collegial advice in programming work that improves learning;
– Initiating practice change in response to need;
– Initiating policy change accordingly; and
– Utilising outside 'expert' knowledge to trigger change in practice.

DIVISION OF LABOUR: ROLES AND RESPONSIBILITIES – COLLABORATION

Collaboration is regarded a social responsibility. In relation to designated roles and responsibilities, collaboration occurs in the context of decision-making. In this school, the framing, making and taking of decisions is undertaken collectively. Roles and responsibilities within this school's collaborative culture suggest senior staff, *see themselves as part of a huge team really but also understand that they do actually have to lead.* Teachers consider themselves empowered to have a say in the decision-making process.

Collaborative decision-making is influenced by many internal and external school factors such as vision buy-in, teacher empowerment, a learning community focus, pressure to manage workload through shared practice, an ethos of self-governance and self-management, trust and 'readiness' in response to changing situational dynamics. Collaborative decisions, embedded in evidential data, ensure transparency of process. Collaborative decision-making hallmarks the way 'things are done around here'. The vignette selected to illustrate this notion of collaborative decision making was taken from a literacy committee meeting where decision making processes focused on the development of a spelling programme.

Stakeholders' roles and responsibilities varied at this meeting but, as always, communal involvement focused on doing what was best for the school and its students. The principal acted as overseer, ensuring discussed items were financially viable and received support (financial and human). Her knowledge of school systems, stakeholder needs, resource availability and obtaining additional funds from the Ministry proved crucial in establishing a rich information base. She fully supported the deputy principal who facilitated the session. She acknowledged staff willingness to provide time, knowledge and expertise in contributing towards the decision making process.

The deputy principal actively sought the views of others on, for example, resource purchase, future programming of spelling and teacher professional development. In all dialogue, she ensured current student data informed the decision-making process. Collective action was emphasised. For example, the deputy principal provided a spelling plan and sought the views of others in using the plan as a springboard for future planning in keeping with this school's needs. Modification, she emphasised, required collective input. Issues of teaching consistency and ongoing support to ensure success of the programme were clarified with staff.

Teachers contributed their practical knowledge to the decision-making process. By way of follow up, teachers communicated information discussed at the literacy committee meeting to members of their own teams. In teams, further discussion on the topic occurred with representatives reporting back staff views at the next committee meeting.

Decision making, as captured, depicts a sense of collectiveness and inclusion. Decisions are made collaboratively and, although collaboration is an unspoken requirement, there is room to negotiate individual position. As with previous examples, room to express doubt, raise debate and question existing practice is encouraged. A flow of information encourages a community of practice, division of labour, collaborative environment.

DIVISION OF LABOUR: ROLES AND RESPONSIBILITIES – REFLECTIVE PRACTICE

Reflective practice invokes the 'striving to be the best in promoting student learning' vision. Staff roles and responsibilities are tied to ensuring reflective practice is initiated and implemented in ways that ensure high expectations of curriculum delivery in terms of quality. Individual appraisals and systemic reviews are formal ways of initiating reflective practice. Daily conversations present themselves as informal opportunities for reflection.

The push for professionalism underpins all forms of reflection. Legislatively it matters that teachers are systematically appraised, seen to be accountable and that the school has a robust system of supervising practice which engender reflection on practice. Reflective practice is an essential part of risk management that ensures this school continues to be an effective, safe, place for learning. From a division of labour: roles and responsibilities viewpoint, it means that the principal, assisted by the deputy principal, conducts staff appraisals while teachers' structure and manage their own peer reviews. The principal appraises senior managers and is herself appraised by board and/or outside consultants.

DIVISION OF LABOUR: ROLES AND RESPONSIBILITIES – NETWORKING

Networking, covered in the knowledge production and utilisation section, was discussed in terms of learning. In this section, roles and responsibilities receive attention. As it is impossible to present data on all networking connections, this section focuses on roles and responsibilities of the principal and the board of trustees. The principal was selected as she is a central player in all networks and exercises a crucial role in maintaining system efficiency. The board's role provides yet another angle to view how networking in relation to governance builds capacity for improvement. The following vignette captures the principal's knowledge creation role at the governance level of practice:

At all board meetings, monthly reports on matters of school business and education in general are presented by the principal. Correspondence presented relates to Ministry of Education edicts, such as: initiatives concerning employment of social workers, making a difference to student achievement, health issues, legal issues pertaining to suspensions and other miscellaneous information contained in circulars. As a disseminator of information, the principal regularly updates the board on new legislation and current trends in education. This role is crucial in building board capacity. Bringing new information to the board's attention facilitates their learning and a building of collective knowledge within which informed governance decisions can be made. In reporting on school matters, the principal provides information specific to site activity. For example, in one meeting attended, updates on curriculum issues, purchase of keyboards, fun and celebratory events, budgets and staffing were raised for discussion. School knowledge keeps the board in touch with current events. The principal's ability to provide necessary information is crucial in gaining board support, developing positive working networks, building community and advancing a collective knowledge base.

Board members also play their part in establishing networks. During the time spent observing board meetings, the board initiated networks to obtain additional funds, build collegiality and sustain a community spirit. For example, the board chair was observed organising the jubilee celebrations. In her report she drew attention to speakers she had organised, research undertaken in retrieving historical school documents and advertising to promote the event. Board members form committees to facilitate governance responsibilities. The reporting back of information from various committees sustains inter-group board and board/school connectedness.

The board's expanded knowledge base is essential in strengthening their ability to contribute to capacity building for school improvement.

DIVISION OF LABOUR: ROLES AND RESPONSIBILITIES –
SYSTEMIC DEVELOPMENT

As part of a working community, school stakeholders were observed developing systems, processes and structures that maximise delivery of the curriculum. The principal was observed on several occasions initiating systemic change in response to new legislation as this vignette illustrates:

> At a staff meeting, the principal was seen communicating current legislative information on health and safety regulations. This staff meeting was aimed at: updating staff knowledge on new health and safety mandates; reviewing current systems, processes and structures in line with the new legislation; modifying and adapting systems accordingly; and engendering collective buy-in to systemic change. The principal utilised a hands-on teaching approach to ascertain staff knowledge on health and safety protocols in use. She asked staff to contribute ideas towards improving current practice. Actions initiated brought about the following changes to existing health and safety protocols:
> - A health and safety visitors' book was initiated;
> - The staff injuries book was reinstated and placed in the staff room for use by all staff;
> - Student involvement in creating a healthier school environment was discussed; and
> - A review of the health and safety policy was scheduled so new procedural guidelines could be formulated, ratified and endorsed.

As school governors, the board plays a part in systemic development. At board meetings, members provide an independent voice of support and inquiry that encourages deeper reflection of practice from a community perspective. Such input depicts a strong desire to gain a deeper appreciation of what happens in practice. Dialogue that unfolds, as captured in the next vignette, endorses collective and collaborative decision-making in policy construction:

> Principal: 'I recommend we read this together. In this school we make sure we deal with each child in an equitable way'.
>
> Board member 1: 'In the purposes section, item number three is repeated in the guidelines. Can we change this? With the second guideline, how will this happen?'
>
> Principal: 'We have to keep this fairly open ended'.

Board member 2: 'Is that because it covers a lot of things such as children with special abilities?'

Debate on policy guidelines, purposes and procedures continued until understanding and agreement were reached and all parties expressed a need to move on. On agreement, policies were ratified.

Systemic development requires financial management. This aspect of board governance is critical in building school capacity. The board receives funding from the government at a variety of levels: base funding according to decile ranking, roll size and other special characteristics. This funding, termed the Operations Grant, is utilised for curriculum, property, personnel (other than teachers' salaries), special needs, resources and all other items covered by legal requirements. It is the board's responsibility to allocate funds to cover the above expenditures in the best way that it can. Other sources of revenue received from donations (fund raising activities, for example) are also utilised for similar purposes. The board, in accordance with the strategic plan, allocates funds for systemic development.

CONCLUSION: LINKS TO CAPACITY BULDING FOR SCHOOL IMPROVEMENT

In this setting, formal workplace structures and networks resemble a division of labour working paradigm. They are underscored by vision which enhances collaborative decision-making, value debates, vision implementation, monitoring of quality, accountability and a working community ethos. For this to work, power structures tend to be of a flat management type. Senior managers, board, teaching staff, support staff and parents work together for the betterment of the school and its stakeholders. School systems and ways of working encourage shared roles and responsibilities whereby, *channels of communication and procedures are in place and people know exactly where they stand and what's expected.*

THEORY

Capacity Building

This chapter explains capacity building for school improvement through a discussion of four themes that emerge from an analysis of the attributes and practices. First, capacity building is a situated activity embedded in context. The four attributes of vision, stakeholders as change agents, school culture and professional development emphasise the importance of context and the situated nature of resulting practice. Three practices that contribute to capacity building for improvement are: knowledge production and utilisation; a 'switching on' mentality; and division of labour: roles and responsibilities. Second, capacity building is the result of connectedness; meaningful activities that 'promote student learning' through the aforementioned practices which, when combined, engender learning, denote the way things are done around here and promote team work. Systems, structures and processes achieve connectedness at the school's external/internal interface and in practice. Third, capacity building involves effective governance, leadership and management. All three aspects of organisational life are interwoven and encompass what happens in relation to capacity building for school improvement. Fourth, capacity building has outcomes. Outcomes represent desirable future states – individual, collective and systemic – related to purpose. Having outcomes means provision of opportunities for feedback which, when used to inform practice, perpetuate and sustain ongoing cycles of capacity building. All four themes underscore capacity building and provide the basis for a theoretical model as captured in Figure 9.1. In the discussion that follows, each theme is examined from the viewpoint of capacity building.

SITUATED ACTIVITY

Literature suggests schools are nested within layers of society (Dantley, 2005). They are interconnected (Hargreaves & Fink, 2006) and operate as open systems (Lam & Punch, 2001; Pristine & Nelson, 2005) influenced by macro and micro cultural norms. In New Zealand, macro cultural norms of accountability, compliance and improvement align with Ministry of Education's aims of raising student achievement and reducing disparity (Alton-Lee, 2003; MOE, 1999a, 2004) underpinned by the need to demonstrate responsiveness to: diverse cultures and a wide range of needs and aspirations; globalisation; the impact of technology and information; and development of a knowledge-based economy. The Ministry's emphasis on achievement is targeted at: effective teaching for all students; family and community engagement in education; and development of quality providers

(MOE, 2004). A wide range of legislative mandates ensure aims are met in practice. Government policy demands of schools accountability, compliance and improvement. Alongside socio-economic factors of location, such requirements influence what happens in practice and capacity building can be considered a response to macro and micro calls for accountability, compliance and improvement. Macro and micro contexts are not static states of 'being' but change in response to acts of 'doing'. The shifting tensions and opportunities for growth that emerge lends weight to the argument that capacity building results from work undertaken to ensure limitations of context are minimised and opportunities maximised to benefit the school. The importance of capacity building as a situated activity, in this regard, cannot be dismissed.

Managing Tensions – Minimising Limitations and Maximising Opportunities

An organisation does not exist in a vacuum (Dantley, 2005; Hargreaves & Fink, 2006; Lam & Punch, 2001; Pristine & Nelson, 2005). Schools are part of complex systems influenced by macro and micro cultural norms. The literature suggests that the current educational climate driven by neo-liberal, market ideologies promote norms of accountability, compliance and improvement (Boyd, 1998; Codd, 1990; 2005; Hawk & Hill, 1997; Leithwood, 2001). Leithwood (2001) claims this presents practitioners with tensions related to markets, decentralisation, professionalisation and management – government approaches to accountability. Codd (2005) states that overzealous support of managerial ideals and values, together with cultures of performance, produce technical rationality and the pursuit of quality reduced to key performance indicators easily measured and recorded. Robinson et al. (2005) add that freedom to manage does not imply reduced accountability to the government; government priorities remain mandatory but with a shift from inputs and procedures to outputs and outcomes. Moreover, results-orientated accountability is difficult to achieve given board attention to legislative requirements, fiscal responsibilities, health and safety matters and curriculum delivery.

Accountability demands aside, tensions accompany the rhetoric that devolved responsibilities to school boards makes for a more efficient system in meeting school and community needs. For example, Dalin (2005) suggests lay governance in decision-making can compromise professional autonomy; Rae (2005) observes that vital energy of boards, principals and staff are continually diverted away from learning and teaching and capacity building towards fulfilment of managerial task; Timperley et al. (2004) state links between accountability and governance are contentious – board members are expected to, but do not necessarily have adequate knowledge of issues surrounding achievement, target setting and monitoring of progress to hold professionals accountable; and Leithwood (2001) comments that autonomy to govern and manage requires lengthy learning, adjustment, negotiation and cultural change.

Increased demands for accountability and compliance, set within a school improvement paradigm, exert pressure on schools to raise performance. The

Ministry's focus on raising achievement and reducing disparity is embedded in key policy statements and endorsed by reform initiatives (see for example, Alton-Lee, 2003; MOE, 1999a, 2004). In a critique of such policies, Honig and Hatch (2004) attribute their limiting effects to incoherence which, Rae (2005) concedes, loosely connects to classroom concerns for teaching and students and families. Coburn (2003) claims that reforms fail to recognise complex challenges of reaching out broadly while cultivating depth of change. Levin (2001) notes government levers for implementing policy are unlikely to promote improvement automatically but depend on the extent and manner in which reform initiatives are taken up by those they are designed to serve. To create deep and lasting improvement, Elmore (1995) advocates movement away from 'adding on' structures or programmes; Honig and Hatch (2004) suggest crafting coherence; and Barth (1990) advances the 'improvement from within' message. McCauley and Roddick (2001) suggest that school improvement is not straightforward but complex and should not be conceived as a single programme with a uniform set of short term goals.

Adding to the milieu of tensions affecting stakeholders' ability to build capacity are challenges a multi-cultural, low decile location presents. In today's society, schools are increasingly multicultural (Alton Lee, 2003; ERO, 2000; MOE, 2004) required to respond to immediate needs of diverse student/community populations. However, as ERO (2000) explains, respective legislative guidelines appear nebulous with schools experiencing difficulty interpreting goals and ascertaining if equity targets are met. Problems associated with multiculturalism extend beyond that of culture (ERO, 2000). Multicultural schools, generally located in poor socio-economic areas, may experience limited parental involvement and, in some cases, poor governance and management and weak or failed teaching provisions (ERO, 1996, 2006). Robinson et al. (2005), reporting on governance issues in low decile schools, question the ability of boards to contribute to capacity building for school improvement based on limited understanding of role requirements and 'good' governance, lack of firsthand experience of tasks and activities over which they are governing and conceptions of 'good' governance related to quality of relationships that appears focused on communicating appreciation and minimising conflict at the expense of mutual accountability, challenge and capacity building.

Research suggests low decile location factors undermine a school's capacity to improve student learning outcomes. Hawk and Hill (1997), in their AIMHI study, identified selected policies, differing home-school expectations and family related factors as generating learning, health, social, economic and welfare needs. Hawk and Hill conclude that low socio-economic factors have implications on schools and their capacity to improve student learning outcomes.

In today's educational landscape, opportunities for growth and expansion accompany tensions. One positive aspect of the reforms is that schools gain from having a greater say in managing their own affairs (Dalin, 2005). Devolution of authority leads to empowerment and a growing sense of duty to engage in local decision-making. In terms of system-wide improvement, Ministry sponsored initiatives to 'scale up' school sector reforms are awarded acclaim. A cluster approach (MOE, 2004) is said to achieve critical mass of new learning in bounded areas (Coburn, 2003). McCauley and Roddick (2001) note that ongoing Ministry support for schools results in certain benefits: creation of learning cultures, access to a variety of support structures, establishment of positive relationships with the Ministry, other schools and the community, access to additional funds and the purchase of consultants and advisors for extra guidance and support.

In the case study school, stakeholders strive to build capacity by managing tensions; that is, minimising limitations and maximising opportunities to benefit the school. The uniformly appealing 'striving to be the best in promoting student learning' message underpins all activity. Management of tensions means balancing demands of an external environment with collaborative ideals of:
– Building school 'heart';
– Establishing a learning community inclusive of parents;
– Encouraging collective stakeholder involvement in student centred learning;
– Building parents' knowledge base for effective partnerships; and
– Acknowledging and celebrating diversity.
In the discussion that follows, tensions of funding, parental involvement, accountability and compliance, location factors and multiculturalism/biculturalism are examined within a situated perspective. Highlighted is the way this school minimises limitations and maximises opportunities to build capacity that fits context. Although tensions are individually presented, their integrated complexity is not to be discounted. Stakeholders employ multi-faceted strategies to solve problems.

Funding

Funding linked to school improvement contains contradictory messages. Raudenbush (2005) notes increased funding has only marginal impact on the quality of classroom learning and student outcomes. Earl and Lee (1998) claim little direct relationship exists between funding and successful school reform. Other educators and researchers (see Codd, 2005; Hawk & Hill, 1997) maintain that funding shortages impact negatively on school improvement because the funding pro rata formula leads to interschool competitiveness for students. Stakeholders in this study confirm that funding shortfalls limit school improvement. While stakeholders acknowledge the negative effects of limited finances, crafting alternative pathways to raise funds by accessing grants and support of local businesses achieve goals as stated in the strategic plans.

Funding shortfalls have historical antecedents. When the school was experiencing a crisis, negative perceptions and families enrolling their children in neighbouring schools generated a declining roll and subsequent reduction in funding. As part of the improvement drive, energy and time went into creating a safe, attractive, physical environment and marketing this school in positive ways. Attention, devoted to changing this school's perception through improving the physical environment and attention to pedagogy, promoted, over a two year period, a 'moving' school reputation. Although stakeholders' efforts succeeded in achieving a remarkable turnaround, the energy involved was said to be 'hugely exhausting', but, crucial in promoting roll growth and funding; precursors for capacity building.

Despite an improved school image, tensions of a quasi-market, competitive environment continue to be felt. Stakeholders are very much aware that macro cultural norms of school choice and interschool competition can assist or restrict their school's growth. In response, a readiness for change exists. This means marketing the school, advancing authentic messages about school practice, raising additional funds through donations and entrepreneurial activities and scanning the environment for patterns/trends that retain this school's 'cutting edge of knowledge production and utilisation' position. This is a situated response to counteracting tensions of funding. Balancing demands of the market and upholding vision ideals demonstrates negotiation of position to benefit the school. Public demand for 'school choice' means creating this school as a 'school of choice' for all students.

Situated ways of working build capacity for school improvement despite acknowledged shortfalls of funding. Buy-in to Ministry of Education contracts, for example, increases individual, collective and systemic knowledge capacities. Establishment of a 'one day' gifted and talented school on site provides opportunities for staff and students to tap into a knowledge base that 'experts' in the field are able to provide. Adult educational classes for families and after school homework sessions meet the needs of minority groups and community respectively. Additional assistance by bi-lingual tutors bridges the home-school divide for families of different ethnicities. Such examples confirm a situated approach to practice that promotes individual, collective and systemic growth.

Parent Involvement

The Ministry of Education advocates parental involvement in schools as advancing student learning (MOE, 1999a, 2004). McCauley and Roddick (2001) Hawk and Hill, (1997) and Robinson et al. (2005) endorse this viewpoint. Although links between parental involvement and student learning are advanced, barriers or limitations are also noted (see for example, Gold et al., 2005; Hawk & Hill, 1997; Robinson et al., 2005). This school's commitment to building parents' educational and personal knowledge is claimed to increase involvement in student learning. Home-school partnership evenings, parent chat sessions and other formal and informal meetings assist in the transference of knowledge, albeit personal and/or educational, to parents. Community surveys gauge satisfaction levels with site-based programmes designed to increase knowledge. The resulting evidence base informs future goal setting in line with community needs and aspirations. Building parents' knowledge capacities reportedly advances home-school links. The support and empathy that results between parents and school personnel fuels a collective passion in supporting capacity building for school improvement.

The New Zealand context assumes and pursues high levels of parental involvement consistent with the devolution of governance and management to school boards and principals (McCauley & Roddick, 2001). The literature consistently presents this as a source of much tension (see for example, Leithwood, 2001; Robinson et al., 2005; Timperley et al., 2004). In this school, parents share in the decision making process at the governance level of practice. As educational leaders, parents work with staff to facilitate home-school partnerships. They raise funds and provide volunteer assistance in numerous ways. This school is a community of practice where a give and take of information and communal 'hard work' promotes goodwill that builds capacity.

Accountability and Compliance

As noted earlier, Dalin (2005), Robinson et al. (2005), Codd (2005), Rae (2005) and Thrupp and Willmott (2003) note that transference of decision making from the state to schools is accompanied by strengthening government accountability over curriculum, assessment of learning and teaching and professional development. Freedom to manage does not imply reduced accountability (Robinson et al., 2005) rather, as Leithwood (2001) claims, it "increases administrators' accountability to the central district or board office for the efficient expenditure of resources" (p. 223). In addition, Leithwood cautions that school leaders may not be well placed to deal with such huge task expectations; success is heavily dependent on individual attributes that may be severely compromised in settings where a lack of knowledge, skills and experience fail to promote professionalism or improvement. The already complex mix is compounded by compliance demands for increased professionalism from policies directed at teachers' and principals' competencies to "stay abreast of best professional practices" (Leithwood, 2001, p. 225).

In this school, calls for accountability, compliance and improvement are addressed as part of 'good' practice reflective of context. Findings confirm the school has robust systems, collective networks of support and shared or distributed roles and responsibilities that manage situational demands from an improvement perspective. Parents and staff work collaboratively to achieve self-management and self-governance that ensures accountability, compliance and improvement requirements are addressed. Such site based characteristics establish this school as a safe place.

In this setting, staff and parents take their accountability, compliance and improvement roles and responsibilities seriously. For example, the desire to increase knowledge of site-based operations is displayed by trustees justified as supporting staff and effectively managing governance roles and responsibilities. Mutual dependence and shared accountability not only addresses Ministry demands but, also, advances the vision.

Low Decile Socio-economic Factors

This school's decile two ranking places it in a low socio-economic bracket with a unique set of challenges similar to that identified by Hawk and Hill (1997). The claim made by staff is that their work is more demanding because of student

100

management difficulties, family aspects, language issues and lack of home support for student learning. Such issues are confronted regularly. They are seen to limit individual, collective and systemic capacities as extra resources, time and energy are needed to maintain organisational equilibrium and improvement amidst pressures to meet social and community needs.

In this site, challenges of location are not dismissed lightly but addressed in various ways. The school's vision and resulting practices insist on an inclusive community approach to building capacity for improvement. For example, surveying parents to establish need builds an evidence base which deepens staff appreciation of community reality; that is, to confrontations, conflicts and struggle community members face. An operational framework of knowledge input together with an open door policy supports parent partnerships in education. Regular communication ensures information given and received accurately reflects what happens in this school while opportunities to get parents 'on side' increases community goodwill. The practices here affirm the claim made by Driscoll and Goldring (2005) that parents build schools' social, financial and human capital.

Multi-ethnic Issues

This school is a low decile, multicultural primary school and there is open recognition and respect for the different ethnicities that comprise its population. Adherence to vision means policies, practices and curriculum delivery systems are adjusted to encompass cultural diversity. Although events such as shared lunches, cultural activities, chat sessions, home-school partnerships, input from bi-lingual tutors and newsletters translated to reach community groups are attempts to bind people together and develop community spirit, successful integration of all groups is still perceived as difficult. Regardless, an inclusive approach to building community continues to be supported, justified as ultimately benefiting students.

In summary, the literature acknowledges that accountability, compliance, improvement and low-socio-economic factors create tensions that impact on stakeholders' intent on building and sustaining capacity for improvement. In this setting, the existence of tensions is confirmed but equally corresponding management from positions of minimising limitations and maximising opportunities to benefit the school – a situated response. The management of selected tensions presented here serves to illustrate contextual responses by stakeholders to enhance capacity building for school improvement.

Dimensions of a Situated Perspective

Capacity building for school improvement is a constantly evolving construct (Potter, Reynolds, & Chapman, 2002), dependent on external and internal political, cultural and socio-economic drivers for its conception. Processes inherent in capacity construction are hard to define accurately because of shifting dimensions of context (McCauley & Roddick, 2001), compounded by what Harris and Young

(2000) and McCauley and Roddick (2001) claim is poor knowledge about what promotes school effectiveness and improvement.

School stakeholders in this site define capacity building for improvement as a situated activity with corresponding outcomes. For example, at the time the school was reported to be in crisis, capacity building in this early phase of improvement, necessitated:

– The principal prioritising and enacting systemic solutions in response to need;
– Utilisation of outside 'experts' to improve practice;
– Creation and reflection of an evidence base for inquiry into practice;
– Construction and implementation of school vision;
– Creation of opportunities to engage in professional talk; and
– Openness to new ideas with growing motivation to learn and stay current.

External agency input related to:

– Input of content knowledge and pedagogical skills;
– Initiation of reflective practice through professional dialogue;
– Collective sharing of information and generation of a 'working' team ethos; and
– Establishment of consistency of practice through:
– Focused attention on vision;
– Systemic modification and adaptation to situational need; and
– Development of infrastructures to support the work of staff.

Capacity building outcomes related to achieving organisational stability through: buy-in to a common sense of direction, development of a positive, working school culture and creation of a safe learning environment. Outside agency representatives were change agents as site-based knowledge, expertise and skills were lacking. With continued drive for school improvement from the principal and newly appointed deputy principal, an internal capacity for self-governance and self-management strengthened. This was largely due to senior managers' knowledge, skills, expertise, collaborative strategies and networks of support in advancing the work previously accomplished by outside agencies. A working culture, professional development opportunities and staff enthusiasm for change altered school conditions. Capacity building measures expanded to include:

– Building teacher confidence to take risks;
– Pushing the boundaries of practice through engagement in new learning;
– Raised teaching and learning expectations;
– Participation in collective pursuit of capacity building;
– Increased responsiveness to demands for change (external and internal);
– Development of a collaborative, working and learning environment inclusive of parents;
– Ongoing systemic support in response to altered school/stakeholder need; and
– Sustainability of a positive school image.

A single definition fails to capture the essence of capacity building for school improvement over time. A lack of uniformity is ascribed to uniqueness of individual perception, time, situational constraints/opportunities and multiplicity of tasks requiring attention. Capacity building is the result of situated activity where responses to site-based demands for change involve:

- Construction of a grounded, shared, evolving vision;
- Vision informed practice; and
- Management of tensions to benefit the school and its stakeholders.

Capacity building for school improvement is a situated activity with vision at its core. Vision accounts for a set of attributes and practices that are considered to be key elements of capacity building. Attributes and practices have attached political, cultural and socio-economic drivers that depict how things are done around here. Processes involved are far from neutral. Values that underpin vision invoke debate on what is morally right and important to stakeholders. Value debates establish group norms or ways of working that reinforce the 'situatedness' of practice.

As a situated activity, capacity building has an incremental quality. This suggests ongoing attention to actions that continue to protect and advance the interest of the school and its stakeholders. Stakeholder actions and practices that are repeated, shared, have a history and evolve in response to external and internal change demands are seen to manage tensions. Management of tensions involving minimising limitations and maximising opportunities builds capacity for improvement.

CONNECTEDNESS

Connectedness is the development of meaningful relationships in pursuit of activities that 'promote student learning'. Connectedness is a multi-dimensional concept that emerges when all stakeholders (Ministry of Education, outside agencies, businesses, parents, staff and students) support the school's vision. Internal connectedness is achieved through practices of knowledge production and utilisation that generate learning; a 'switching on' mentality that reinforces norms of how things are done around here; and division of labour to provide for shared roles and responsibilities that advances team work – collaboration in getting things done. Findings from this study reveal an inevitable connection to *The National Education Guidelines* because of statutory links that connect the school's vision to government legislative guidelines. School documents, systems, processes and structures promote external/internal links with beneficial flow-on effects in practice. In the following sections, the concept of connectedness is explained by considering what happens at the external/internal school interface and the contributions made by each of the three practices.

Connectedness at the External/Internal Interface

Connectedness at the external/internal interface occurs on several levels with benefits to the school and its stakeholders. First, addressing mandated requirements means the school meets health and safety standards (ERO, 2005). In addition, implementation of new legislation sustains a 'safe place' ethos that participants note is conducive to learning. Second, the Ministry of Education, outside agencies, tertiary institutions, schools and other community groups serve as catalysts for change through provision of new information. Opportunities to participate in

Ministry contracts and buy-in of outside agency support for curriculum and pedagogical development is reported as advancing individual, collective and systemic 'working' knowledge capacities. Similar claims are made of association with professional networks. The claim made by school stakeholders is that outside knowledge raises standards of expectations, motivates learning and leads to new, more effective ways of doing things. The value of outside connections in improving teacher content knowledge and pedagogical skills is acknowledged by various authors (see for example, Phillips et al., 2001; Symes et al., 2001; Timperley & Robinson, 2001). Third, connectedness with the Ministry, outside agencies and community groups bolsters the school's working resource base. For example: Ministry facilitators and outside agency representatives were observed assisting staff to develop systems, processes and structures to suit altered work arrangements; additional funds from the Ministry meant continuation of support structures such as the bi-lingual tutors' initiative; and parental involvement in school life was seen to reduce work load.

Internal/external connectedness achieves 'crafted coherence' (see Honig & Hatch, 2004) where, "ongoing investments in the institutional capacity of schools and district central offices to engage in practices ... help schools manage multiple external demands productively" (p. 27). Crafting coherence is a connected, situated activity as the school seeks assistance and exercises control over its improvement trajectory. School stakeholders negotiate scope of support needed to achieve goals. In other words, connectedness and situated activity promotes meaningful relationships in activities that 'promote student learning'. The discussion that follows explains site-based development of meaningful relationships in pursuit of 'promoting student learning' through practices of knowledge production and utilisation, a switching on mentality and division of labour: roles and responsibilities.

Connectedness through Knowledge Production and Utilisation

Literature suggests professional development raises teacher professionalism (MOE, 1999a; 2000) and initiates school improvement (see for example, Alton-Lee, 2003; Barth, 1990; Day & Sachs, 2004; Elmore, 2002; Fullan & Mascall, 2000). In addition, learning is best achieved through collaborative forms of professional development where social processing of knowledge encourage teachers to work and talk to one another on issues of improving practice (see for example, Annan et al., 2003; Barth, 1990; Duncombe & Armour; 2004; Wenger, McDermott, & Snyder, 2002). In this school, professional development strategies that initiate social processing of knowledge include: collaborative interchange, reflection on practice, openness to new ideas and management of professional development to ensure relevancy, flexibility and scaffolded learning. Strategies ensure teacher learning connects to student learning and effective practice. The result is systemic coherence, consistency of practice and development of a professional learning community. Professional development that focuses attention on tangible outcomes as stated in reviews and strategic plans facilitates learning that meets individual, collective and systemic need within a social constructivist framework.

The professional development package on offer in this school is best defined as a situated, layered approach to learning with connections at the individual, collective and school level of practice. Attention relates to ensuring the individual, collective and system connects to preferred ways of working; that is, in teams with shared responsibility for task achievement. For this to happen, new ideas are introduced at a collective staff level and developed in teams and amongst individuals to create meaning and purpose. The learning that eventuates is specific to context. Situated, layered learning, a product of shared responsibility in task completion, creates connectedness. For example, collective construction of unit plans encourages conversations on teaching and learning among group members. Knowledge generation and the learning that results enhances systemic coherence, consistency of practice and a learning enriched environment which, Rosenholtz (1989) claims, creates motivation for learning as a daily activity. A situated, layered approach facilitates connectedness because:

- New knowledge, added to an existing tacit knowledge base, increases individual, collective and systemic depth of content and pedagogical knowledge/understanding;
- Monitoring of practice (systemic and individual) ensures learning has the potential to reach the classroom level of practice to benefit students;
- Scaffolded learning opportunities create opportunities for feedback which reportedly improves practice (see Knight, 2003); and
- The approach to learning is community based. This ensures parents are part of the holistic drive to improve delivery of the curriculum.

An attitude of 'openness to new ideas' prevails in this setting. 'Openness to new ideas' reflects a mentality that endorses connection with outside sources of knowledge. Ministry of Education contracts are valued for their potential to expand individual, collective and systemic knowledge in specified curriculum areas. The same can be said of one-day workshops and conference attendance. Although one-day workshops are critiqued for promoting a narrow perception of change (Boyle, Lamprianou, & Boyle, 2004), decontextualised (Duncombe & Armour, 2004) and passive learning (Fullan & Mascall, 2000), staff who attend one-day workshops or conferences return with knowledge to share. Through reflective practice and dialogue, they assist others to experiment with new ideas. Outsider information transferred to context places this school and its stakeholders at the cutting edge of new knowledge development and continuously enforced is the concept of connectedness and group ways of working that expand individual, collective and systemic knowledge bases. Learning in this site is situated and learning frameworks constructed are based on authenticated need. Situated activity and connectedness means:

- Everyone is considered a learner, a leader, a catalyst for change and a change agent;
- Opportunities for professional development promote lifelong learning mindsets;

- Mutual respect and trust facilitate the raising of doubt and the asking of 'hard questions' to alter habits and beliefs concerning teaching and learning;
- Collective dialogue and reflection generates knowledge at individual, collective and systemic levels of practice; and
- Attention is always on 'striving to be the best in promoting student learning'.

Connectedness through a 'Switching on' Mentality

Deal and Kennedy (1982; 1983) define culture as 'the way we do things around here'. Beare, Caldwell and Millikan (1989) refer to culture as verbal, behavioural and visual manifestations enacted in practice. Schein (1985) defines the concept as, "basic assumptions and beliefs that are shared by members of an organisation, that operate unconsciously, and that define in a basic 'taken-for-granted' fashion an organisation's view of itself and its environment" (p. 6). Embedded in these comments is the importance of symbolic, practical, linguistic and interpersonal relationships of setting that create connectedness.

In this school, cultural hallmarks that emerge from actions, behaviours and expectations of stakeholders identify how things are done around here. They denote aspects of school life that are important. Cultural hallmarks espoused and enacted draw attention to a learning culture, an inclusive culture, collaboration, commitment, community and a safe place. Cultural hallmarks create a school identity that connect and bind people together to aspects of practice that are valued. For example, stakeholders in this school connect with and value learning. Valuing learning means engineering time and place for collective dialogue or learning talk to occur. Such comments are frequently expressed in support: *we want children to come in and be switched on to learning, have a desire to learn* and *developing learners for the future is important.* Valuing learning and stakeholder involvement in the learning process generates a professional learning community which promotes and sustains the learning of all stakeholders. A professional learning community is conducive for capacity building as endorsed by the literature (Bolman et al., 2005; Stoll et al., 2006).

In this school, respect for multiculturalism is evident in the verbal, behavioural and visual manifestations of culture. It generates an inclusive 'family' ethos. 'Family' denotes celebration of cultural diversity as "unique systems of perceiving and organising the world" (Helu-Thaman, 2003, p. 120). Values of tolerance, fairness, caring or compassion, non-sexism and non-racism underpin the 'family' ethos. In practice this means school systems, processes and structures are geared towards achieving outcomes for all students. Acceptance and celebration of diversity and displays of cultural sensitivity are interwoven into practice. The family ethos draws different stakeholder groups together in supporting this school.

The value of collaborative cultures in facilitating school improvement is endorsed by many authors (see for example, Hargreaves, 1994; Hopkins et al., 1994; Nias et al., 1989). In this school, a culture of collaboration fosters team work and community spirit. The principal, senior managers, teaching and non-teaching staff and parents are described as team players. Their participatory actions endorse togetherness in goal achievement. School systems, processes and structures support collaboration as, for example, in creating opportunities for collective dialogue and collaborative decision-making. In the spirit of collaboration, connectedness is achieved through task completion which demands mutual dependence and professional interdependencies. A culture of collaboration is, as Hargreaves (1991, cited in Hopkins et al., 1994) describes: spontaneous, voluntary, development oriented, pervasive across time and space and unpredictable. In this school such a culture achieves connectedness among all in the building of capacity for school improvement. Individuals espouse and enact commitment to the collective. Commitment builds trust in people to act professionally as individuals and within a collective. Group ways of working account for distributed practice (Gronn, 2002), mutual trust (Codd, 2005), empowerment and networks of support (Muijs & Harris, 2003). All aspects create a safe environment where meaningful relationships and expression of voice and opinion are encouraged. Here, thinking through issues as a collective promotes joint 'ways of doing things'. Stakeholders are encouraged to grow through expression of voice. The culture of this school fits a moving school description (Hargreaves, 1995) where optimal social cohesion and high expectations create a 'switching on' mentality and connectedness.

Connectedness through Division of Labour: Roles and Responsibilities

In this school, connectedness occurs through working in teams. For example, educational leadership is not just the prerogative of those in positions of authority but shared amongst others. Educational leadership denotes aspects of distributed practice (see for example, Gronn, 2002; Harris, 2004), teacher leadership (York-Barr & Duke, 2004) and parallel leadership (Andrews & Crowther, 2002). The general feeling is that team work achieves more. As captured in the mission statement: '*I can do it you can do it and together we can achieve our goals*', team work is an enacted group norm exercised at all levels of practice.

At the governance level of practice, board and staff enter into accountability partnerships. Current research by Timperley et al. (2004) and Robinson et al. (2005) indicate that lack of knowledge and understanding of school issues limits board involvement and contribution towards capacity building. In this site, board capacity for effective governance is enhanced through team work. Board members engage in information sharing, collective dialogue and collaborative decision-making which builds mutual trust, respect and connectedness to the school and each other. Team work at the board level enhances:

- Collaboration in meeting accountability, compliance and improvement demands;
- Opportunities for individual/collective representation;
- Development of an eclectic knowledge base for decision-making;
- Team spirit;
- Collective dialogue and participatory decision-making;
- A valuing of interdependence amongst members;
- Promotion of trust and learning;

– Systemic coherence and consistency of practice; and
– As Nias et al. (1989) note, relationships that "are tough and flexible enough to withstand shocks and uncertainties from within and without" (p. 74).

Shared task accomplishment epitomises teamness among staff in advancing effective school functioning. Distributed practice is evident throughout the school. For example, teacher leadership ensures the improvement agenda is grounded. Involvement in decision-making increases self-efficacy and high levels of morale (see York-Barr & Duke, 2004). All staff are strategic thinkers. Their roles and responsibilities are crucial in sustaining capacity for improvement.

Parental involvement contributes to connectedness in practical ways. Parents:
– Raise funds;
– Engender community involvement in education and school life through home-school partnerships;
– Provide educational leadership in cultural group activities;
– Advance the profile of the school through community networks; and
– Assist staff in daily activities.

To summarise, connectedness is a multi-dimensional construct. It concerns the development of meaningful relationships in pursuit of activities that 'promote student learning'. Connectedness to *The National Education Guidelines* is inevitable. Mandated guidelines, addressed in practice, promote this school as a safe place for learning. A systemic approach ensures connectedness at the external/internal interface and in practice. Internal connectedness is achieved through practices of knowledge production and utilisation, a 'switching on' mentality and division of labour into shared roles and responsibilities. Connectedness is directly linked to situated activity and as such can be considered an underpinning theme of capacity building for school improvement.

GOVERNANCE, LEADERSHIP AND MANAGEMENT

Capacity building for school improvement requires effective governance, leadership and management. Governance, leadership and management inevitably means meeting accountability, compliance and improvement demands as stipulated in *The National Education Guidelines*. In this school, stakeholders are aware of their roles and responsibilities aligned to meeting government mandates and to each other. They manage calls for accountability, compliance and improvement as individuals and within a collective to maintain organisational equilibrium and advance improvement. Stakeholders work as change agents to build capacity for improvement by exercising:
– Visionary leadership;
– Educational leadership;
– Network building; and
– Systemic development.

Stakeholders are guardians of the vision. As vision guardians, they perpetuate its construction. Their input keeps the vision alive and grounded in reality. Vision renewal is not imposed but created from practice; not isolated but part of everyday life; and planned in terms of initiating growth and development. The '*I can do it, you can do it and together we can achieve our goals*' statement enhances collective buy-in to vision. Stakeholders are forever mindful of avoiding the 'blunting of vision' (Barth, 1990) effect with respect to tensions of context. 'Blunting of vision' is minimised by working towards vision in thoughtful, planned and collective ways. Stakeholders ensure that vision ideals permeate through all levels of practice to promote student learning. Vision is embedded in this school's culture and its implementation monitored and reinforced through governance, management and leadership activities. Collective construction of vision raises communal consciousness to its implementation. Stakeholders' espousal and enactment of values and beliefs create cultural hallmarks that assist in vision implementation. Internalisation and continued enactment of cultural hallmarks make stakeholders, in governance, leadership and management capacities, agents of change recreating what they believe to be moral and ethical practice.

As signalled and discussed previously, all stakeholders provide educational leadership. The board endorses professional development through allocation of funds in accordance with stated goals contained in strategic plans. The professional development agenda is driven by staff. Their engagement in individual and systemic reviews creates base line data from which to construct learning trajectories. Staff engagement in monitoring of professional development increases their professionalism. In this school, educational leadership draws on skills and abilities of all stakeholders. To quote from Fitzgerald and Gunter's (2006) study, "The leadership of learning is not necessarily undertaken solely by those with formal responsibility that is denoted by a title or label" (p. 53). The culture, best described as a professional learning community draws on all as educational leaders and learners to enhance the building of capacity for school improvement.

In this school, many forms of formal/informal and internal/external networks exist to support community life. A flat management structure promotes networking and team work and team arrangements serve as powerful structures to push for capacity building. Networking and team work in governance, leadership and management capacities offers:

– Access to information from which to engage in knowledge creation;
– Access to systemic and collegial support;
– Engagement in processes of participatory decision-making;
– Opportunities to consult and negotiate future plans as a collective;
– Engagement in value debates;
– Ability to meet accountability, compliance and improvement demands in collective ways;
– Opportunities to attach meaning and purpose to work;
– Opportunities to solve problems and deal with conflict in creative ways; and
– Opportunities to build and sustain coherency in accordance with purpose.

All stakeholders with governance, leadership and management roles and responsibilities are system developers. Systemic development is achieved through distributed practice. This is a school where school structures are 'regularised' to promote sharing of practice (Gronn, 2002). The overall school structure promotes teamness as preferred ways of working but not at the expense of professional autonomy. Work here is, as Sayles (1964) describes it, "coordinated and undertaken interdependently" (p. 115). Individuals contribute to a collective knowledge base that is of pragmatic use in systemic development. A systemic approach values both individual and collective contribution to school capacity building for improvement.

Systemic development requires leadership qualities of governors, leaders and managers which are transformational (see for example, Northhouse, 2004) and post-transformational (see for example, Day, 2000; Fullan, 2002; Sergiovanni, 2006; West et al., 2000). In addition, distributed leadership practices, as defined by Gronn (2002), and management practices, as purported by Dalin (2005) and Hallinger and Snidvongs (2005), are required. The demand for inclusive approaches to governance, leadership and management (see for example, Furman & Shields, 2005; Lindsey, Roberts & Cambell Jones, 2005; Shields & Sayani, 2005) coupled with calls to develop a professional learning community (see for example, Barth, 1990; Bolman et al., 2005; Stoll et al., 2006) are also frequently raised. Observation of practice suggests that a systemic approach receives the attention of stakeholders in performing the multitude of tasks expected of them. School systems, processes and structures ensure decisions made collectively serve the best interest of the school and its stakeholders. A systemic approach offers best 'fit' with conditions of context (external and internal). Systemic development draws on all stakeholders' support in sustaining school improvement.

CAPACITY OUTCOMES

Outcomes are inherent in all capacity building activities. Outcomes are traceable to the vision statement – 'striving to be the best in promoting student learning' and inevitably, to *The National Education Guidelines*. Participants' comments indicate that being 'the best' is multi-dimensional and having outcomes contribute towards:
– Working towards vision and support of the four tenets;
– Provision of a balanced curriculum that addresses the diverse needs of students;
– Development of a professional learning culture inclusive of all stakeholders;
– Creating practices in support of biculturalism and multiculturalism;
– Competing favourably with other schools in promoting roll growth;
– Effective management of tensions;
– Promotion of this school as 'school of choice';
– Productive partnerships between staff and parents;
– Connectedness among all parties in doing what is best for the school; and
– Systemic coherence and consistency of practice.

Capacity building has both process and product outcomes related to specific practices of knowledge production and utilisation, switching on mentality and division of labour into shared roles and responsibilities. Commonly associated outcomes for all practices include:
– Focused attention on promoting student learning;
– Reinforcement of the tenets in support of the vision ideal;

– Doing the ordinary things better;
– Maintaining a sense of equilibrium coupled with that of improvement;
– Building on past endeavours to meet current and future needs; and
– Promoting this school as a safe place.

Outcomes are a necessary part of organisational existence for both legislative and internal reasons. However, Busher's (2006) comments on the multifaceted nature of outcomes indicate that only some are relatively easy to measure. Furthermore, although governments place importance on academic attainment of students, "it is the other outcomes – people's personal, social, physical, aesthetic and moral developments – that are more important and of greater consequence in shaping ... adult lives" (p. 2). The point Busher makes is valid when making judgement calls on what builds capacity for improvement through recourse to outcomes.

This school has robust systems, processes and structures that monitor, collate, analyse and utilise data in improving practice. Outcomes related to student progress are measured and reported in accordance with mandatory requirements. Results depict the school as complying with *The Education Guidelines* and the Ministry's broad aims of raising achievement and reducing disparity. This school does, however, have outcomes that are more holistic in nature as noted in successive strategic plans. The concern, therefore, is how to measure the effect of vision, culture and professional development to promote school improvement and, specifically, to advance student learning.

This school's philosophy of 'promoting student learning' means that all aspects of organisational life are scrutinised in an attempt to improve practice. To authenticate effectiveness of vision, school culture and professional development on improving practice that is more than just an account of 'feel', attention is paid to staff accounts of their personal and professional growth reflective of context. It is in the telling of stories and collaborative interchanges or dialogue that change of practice gets acknowledged. As sustainability of improvement is important, judgements calls that indicate improvement to practice are gained through talking to people and:

– Observation of practice;
– Individual appraisals;
– Self-reflection; and
– Systemic reviews that generate a collective data base.

In any capacity building endeavour, recourse to establishing, monitoring and evaluating outcomes matter in building capacity for school improvement. There is a need to acknowledge the need for change. In this site, outcomes are collectively decided and recorded in school documents such as strategic plans. Systems of monitoring, recording and reporting on outcomes promote a sense of rigour to the claim that this school does indeed 'strive to be the best in promoting student learning'. Outcomes related to measuring student data (so called hard data) generally fall into more measurable categories than those attached to change of culture, implementation of vision and teacher professional growth and development (so called soft data). Measurement of both data types is undertaken to

determine overall school improvement. In all forms of measurement, attention is given to utilising evidential data to record:
- Starting points for change;
- Outcomes in response;
- Steps taken to achieve outcomes;
- Monitoring and evaluation of the journey towards improvement; and
- Future planning in response to need.

A THEORETICAL MODEL OF CAPACITY BUILDING FOR SCHOOL IMPROVEMENT

Capacity building for school improvement is a difficult concept to define. Hopkins et al. (1998) define it as enabling conditions that allow process to affect product. Enabling conditions refer to staff development, enquiry and reflection on progress, involvement of students in the teaching and learning process, distributed leadership, collaborative planning and coordinated school-wide activity that establishes coherence. Fullan (2005) suggests the construct relates to development of collective ability to act together to bring about change. Stoll et al. (2006) link the construct to sustainable school improvement best achieved in professional learning communities. They define capacity building as a "complex blend of motivation, skill, positive learning, organisational conditions and culture, and infrastructure of support ... (that) gives individuals, groups, whole school communities and school systems the power to get involved in and sustain learning over time" (p. 221).

These definitions do not fully position or capture the complexity of the construct in context. Context in itself is a multi-dimensional concept that requires deconstruction. Schools are embedded in external (macro) and internal (micro) contexts within which capacity building for school improvement eventuates. Both external and internal contexts exert influence on how the construct is conceived. Values, beliefs and norms of an external context, coupled with those of an internal context, influence a particular brand of capacity building with specific improvement outcomes. Capacity building, therefore, can be considered an act of making informed choices and being able to justify the choices made. Making choices in a landscape filled with competing values and beliefs create tensions for stakeholders' intent on building capacity for school improvement.

New Zealand schools operate within external and internal contexts influenced by society and a national education system, in particular. Macro cultural norms of accountability, compliance and improvement and socio-economic location factors are influences and shape what happens in schools. They determine what is of value. Macro and micro values provide a framework within which vision construction occurs. This school's vision is an act of deliberate choice. The school's vision is encapsulated in a powerful message – 'striving to be the best in promoting student learning'. The vision ideal is supported by four tenets: student centred learning, improvement mindset, empowerment and community. The

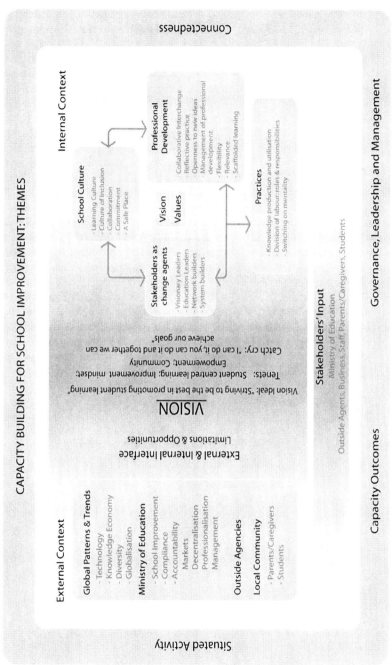

Figure 9.1 Capacity Building for School Improvement – A Theoretical Model

particular way the school defines and works towards making vision a reality creates a distinctive brand of capacity building for school improvement.

The theory of capacity building for improvement advocated in this book places vision at the hub of the model (see Figure 9.1). Vision is considered an attribute along with stakeholders as change agents, school culture and professional development. All four attributes determine the nature of practice. An examination of data reveals three key practices as important. These include knowledge production and utilisation, a 'switching on' mentality and division of labour: roles and responsibilities. A detailed examination of attributes and practices reveal four themes that underscore capacity building for school improvement. These are: situated activity; connectedness; governance leadership and management; and outcomes. Capacity building for school improvement is a situated activity, embedded in context. It also requires connectedness explained as meaningful relationships in support of activities that 'promote student learning'. Stakeholders' governance, leadership and management attributes, skills, roles and responsibilities set the parameters for practice. All three are essential in ensuring the construct is well conceived and inclusive of all stakeholders. Outcomes reflect the situated nature of context and reflection and feedback into practice promotes ongoing cycles of capacity building for school improvement.

The process of building capacity is complex. In this school, all four themes form the basis of a substantive theory; a theoretical model of capacity building for school improvement. Combined they underscore how stakeholders of this school build capacity for improvement. Figure 9.1 captures the complexity of the construct and interconnection among all components to explain how capacity building for school improvement eventuates.

END PIECE

This research found that strong networks among Ministry, outside agencies and school stakeholders, at local and national levels, provided important input for the sustainment and further development of capacity building for improvement. Such networks enabled this school to manage tensions and issues of context in line with vision. It is important, in light of the findings, that schools feel reassured that building capacity for school improvement is not an isolated venture but support and assistance from external agencies contributes to success. In other words, networking and building micro/macro level connections meet individual, collective and systemic needs to enhance capacity building for improvement.

Networking and a commitment to assisting schools on an individual basis require full acknowledgement and support from the Ministry of Education and outside agencies. As Honig and Hatch (2004) note "ongoing processes where schools and central agencies work together to manage external demands" (p. 27) challenges the stereotypical role of policy makers as primary decision makers, replacing them with supportive roles for schools and their decisions. The Ministry and outside agencies need to be more open to suggestions from school stakeholders as to what works in building capacity in context. A situated, connected response to highly complex issues of context, sustain and strengthen a school's capacity for improvement.

In light of the research findings, the school's vision forms the core of all capacity building for school improvement activities. In terms of its construction, the vision engenders passion, purpose and movement in the one direction. Working with vision promotes purpose driven action that buffers and protects the school from undue demands for change. Although the power of vision is central, there is a need to deconstruct the ideal and express it in practical terms so as to achieve a 'blueprint' for action and attach meaning to work. It is imperative, therefore, to consider how documentation, policies, procedures and management systems connect with vision and corresponding values if authentic capacity building for school improvement is to be achieved. An implication for boards of trustees, school managers, teachers and parents is to focus specifically on articulating clearly their school's vision and implementing it in ways that develop congruence between philosophy, values, sense of purpose and practice.

Current educational trends present major challenges for school stakeholders desirous of capacity building for school improvement. Some ideas espoused by the 'new right' ideology, however, appear to sit comfortably alongside capacity building for school improvement. For example, the need for efficiency, effectiveness and accountability can be argued as essential capacity drivers. The goal of building community and partnerships is equally well placed here. Indeed, as the data reveals, such concepts underpin this school's vision and are vital in building its sound capacity base. Given this, however, it is essential that school stakeholders continue to adopt a critical stance to what drives them in, for example, vision construction. Furthermore, whilst it is important to 'take on board' key aspects the 'new right' ideology proposes, the philosophy that binds and drives the capacity building process must be the ideal. Core messages, such as, 'striving to be the best in promoting student learning', must be expressed and modelled despite pressures to accommodate any market approaches to education.

There is a need for each school to ensure that its core philosophy, values and beliefs are fully integrated in school life to form a culture supportive of improvement. For example, contradictions between what is articulated and enacted may serve to negate the capacity building for school improvement process. For boards of trustees and staff this necessitates evaluating the culture of the school, the quality of interpersonal relationships and ascertaining the degree to which both contribute to capacity building for school improvement. If all school stakeholders are to be held responsible for assisting in capacity building for school improvement, then all should be involved in periodic reviews of the school's culture and offered assistance on how to support the building of capacity for improvement. It is also important that new staff, board members and parents have regular opportunities to 'come on board' by developing their knowledge and understanding of systems, processes and structures. A system that enables new school stakeholders to learn about the school through others may help avoid any future misconceptions and conflict from developing.

Professional development that is simply focused on expanding individual teacher's repertoire of classroom practice is not adequate in building capacity for school improvement. Professional development has to contain elements of increasing institutional as well as collective and individual application. Collaborative forms of professional development, a situated, layered approach and a learning community culture allows stakeholders opportunities to discuss beliefs about teaching and learning, critique their own and others' practice, take risks and share in processes of knowledge production and utilisation. The learning that results connects stakeholders to a situation with outcomes aligned to purpose. Learning, albeit individual, collective and/or systemic, is transformative. Such practices must be encouraged in context to build capacity for school improvement.

Findings from this study indicate that parents are involved in capacity building for school improvement in a variety of ways. For example, parents, through the board of trustees, bring a community perspective to matters of governance. Other parent groups, such as 'Friends of the School' and ethnic groups offer support in terms of fund raising and cultural activities. All activities are pathways that promote situated, connected outcomes and focused practice in the building of capacity. However, if increasing parental involvement in school life is desirous and the preservation and honouring of the true meaning of partnership is required, then, schools and educational leaders must critically assess issues that negate any or all of the above. A deeper understanding of issues such as those associated with low socio-economic factors, communication difficulties among the ethnic groups, lack of time and energy to get involved and perpetuated myths about school life, is needed. Maintaining a critical perspective to building authentic partnerships may add to the pressures and tensions schools already face in building capacity for school improvement. In light of the research findings, however, further research into nature, type and purpose of parental involvement at both the micro-level by individual schools and at a macro-level by educational authorities is deemed necessary to provide a more authentic take on the rhetoric 'parents as partners in the education of their children'. Without valid information, the rhetoric is liable to perpetuate unchallenged and the true value of partnership may fail to be established.

RESOURCE

Methodology

The research employed a case study design that was both instrumental (Stake, 1994) and explanatory (Yin, 2003). The inquiry focused on achieving depth of understanding in a single case purposefully selected. As Patton (1990) explains, 'The logic and power of purposeful sampling lies in selecting *information-rich cases* for study ... those from which one can learn a great deal about issues of central importance to the purposes of the research' (p. 169, italics in the original). This study asked the following questions:

1. How was capacity building for school improvement defined – what are its features?
2. How do internal school factors – vision, stakeholder activity, culture and professional development – evolve capacity?
3. In what ways do external wider societal factors influence the development of capacity?
4. What links exist between capacity building and improvement as evidenced in this school setting?

The school selected was a state primary school located in Auckland, New Zealand. It was a contributing (Year 1-6) school with a decile two ranking. At the time of data collection, the roll was approximately 330 with just over 20 teachers. Its ethnic composition included: New Zealand European, 16%; Samoan, 14%; Tongan, 11%; Indian, 11%; Maori, 10%; Ethiopian, 6%; Somalian, 5%; Niuean, 4%; Cook Island, 4% and "other", 19% (Education Review Office (ERO) report, 2005). The low socio-economic background of many students combined with an influx of refugee migrant families presented this school with challenges in, for example, curriculum delivery and responding to diversity.

Over a two year period, the school received much acknowledgement for its capacity to improve. The ERO (2005) report claimed students expressed pride in their school, met high expectations set for them, benefited from a wide range of learning and cultural experiences, engaged in positive student-staff relationships and took advantage of opportunities to participate in school-wide decision making. Further, a professional learning culture existed. Such factors made the school an information rich case within which to conduct this research.

FIELDWORK AND DATA COLLECTION

The fieldwork phase of data collection extended over a twelve month period and mainly included interviews, observations at staff and team meetings and document analysis. In addition, on-going journal entries and photographs recorded participants' stories, experiences and descriptive accounts of actions and conditions connected with practice. Journal entries enhanced interpretation of data commensurate with early analysis and gradual emergence of theory.

Use of grounded theory methods meant field work could not be confirmed in advance. Design flexibility related to the open-ended nature of this inquiry and a pursuit of understanding complexity. Patton (1990) endorses this as doing what makes sense and reporting, "fully on what was done, why it was done, and what the implications are for findings" (p. 62). Data collection focused on:

- Processes, systems and structures that built capacity – an examination of practice;
- Frequency, type and nature of outside agency input;
- Parent involvement in line with inquiry aims;
- Professional development and processes for knowledge production and utilisation. This included knowledge management with the potential to change practice;
- Description, purpose, quality and nature of stakeholder interaction around practice; and
- Group norms that underpinned and defined 'work' in this school.

Interviews conducted included individual in-depth interviews, informal interviews by way of conversations and group interviews. Individual interviews initiated thought and appropriated an overall sense of direction. School participants interviewed were: three senior managers (principal, deputy principal and assistant principal); three senior teachers with syndicate responsibilities; eight classroom teachers; two specialist teachers; four teacher aides; and two support staff. Participant selection resulted from employing purposive sampling techniques (Patton, 1990). Participants invited to participate had been involved in initiating school improvement over a three year period, had experienced school change and represented different levels of school organisation (junior, middle and senior) with various roles and responsibilities. Four parents, two board members and four representatives from outside agencies were also interviewed. Participant selection here was also purposefully determined in line with inquiry aims.

Unscheduled interviews assumed the form of informal conversations or chats, valued for their ability to clarify points and connect with incidents that occurred during the day. Informal conversations provided valuable feedback on unfolding situational events (Patton, 1990). This increased the relevance of events observed. The spontaneity and flexibility with which these interviews occurred provided a means to follow up on leads.

Two group interviews were held with the senior management team and bilingual support workers. Senior managers were asked to consider the journey the school had taken towards improvement over a three year period. The bilingual group were asked to discuss practices that accommodated cultural differences and supported programmatic change.

In this inquiry, observations heightened sensitivity towards patterns of behaviour. Participant and non-participant observations were employed but on different occasions and for different purposes. Participant observations were conducted at home-school events such as the Fun Fiesta night and provided opportunities to observe collective activity that generates capacity. Non-participant observations at negotiated school, team and literacy professional development meetings evidenced interconnections among individuals and groups, teacher talk, negotiation, decision making processes and systemic and structural change that advanced the acquisition and dissemination of knowledge to reach all levels of the school. Non-participant observations at board of trustees meetings, cultural groups, home-school partnership and 'parent chat' meetings provided opportunities to witness community contributions to the knowledge production and utilisation process.

Systematic analysis of documents such as curriculum reviews, strategic plans, charters, ERO reviews, policy manuals and school newsletters provided:
- An impression of patterns and key features of practice;
- Evidence of conditional pathways of influence from critical events/incidents to practice; and
- Corroborated 'other' evidence related to capacity building.

GROUNDED THEORY METHODS FOR DATA ANALYSIS

Use of grounded theory methods suited this inquiry as capacity building for school improvement has little or no prior investigation and applicable conceptual frameworks are unavailable within which to investigate the phenomenon (Strauss & Corbin, 1998). Glaser and Strauss' (1967) stance on theory building, that is, 'construction' of theory through discovery, was considered particularly apt.

Grounded theory methods, noted for their rigour, provided a systematic way of constructing a substantive theory. Here, microanalysis or line by line examination of data proved advantageous in developing open and axial codes (Strauss & Corbin, 1998). Microanalysis encouraged close listening to participants' voices to understand how certain events were interpreted. It allowed *in vivo* codes to surface and guide the naming of categories. It generated 'Who?', 'What?', 'Where?', 'When?', 'Why?' and 'How?' questions of properties, dimensions and conditions, giving emerging categories and sub-categories greater explanatory power (Strauss & Corbin, 1998).

Initial open coding of raw data produced copious quantities of codes. Continual verification and subsequent modification, saturation and placement of each code in relationship to other codes had the desired effect of slowing the process down. Coded elements were organised into categories together with their sub-categories. Here, memo writing proved useful as a way of guiding, tracking and, as Strauss (1987) notes, '(moving) the analyst further from the data into a more analytic realm' (p.32). Memos highlighted ideas, hunches and new insights. Category names were derived from the literature, taken directly from the substantive field by way of *in vivo* codes and sourced from the researcher's professional and theoretical knowledge and experience.

Following open coding of the data, rearrangement into axial codes added greater conceptual depth to the analysis. Questions such as: 'Who?', 'What?', 'Where?', 'When?', 'Why?', 'How?' and 'With what consequences?' invoked responses that further illuminated relationships. An interview-observation data schedule that represented categories and sub-categories across all data sets was developed.

Open and axial coding preceded selective coding. Here the core and causal categories of capacity building were clarified on the basis of:
- Centrality and frequency of mention;
- Natural connection to other categories;
- Accommodation of properties that varied; and
- Descriptions of participants' main concern (Glaser, 1978).
- In addition to the above, Strauss and Corbin's (1990) paradigm model helped sharpen explanations of processes, relationships and the influence of context on practice.

Data analysis began with the initial analysis of interview transcripts followed by analysis of observational and documentation data. Every unit of data was coded and grouped into tentative categories and subcategories using the following process. The first interview transcript was read to ascertain data that appeared significant. A second reading of the same transcript prompted the underlining of key phrases, words or sentences that had deliberate bearing on the concept. Continuous questioning in the form of, 'What is this?', 'What does this mean?' initiated more thoughts and ideas. Summary notes, made in the margin of the transcript, formed preliminary codes. Keeping in mind these codes had emerged from the first transcript, the process was applied to other interview transcripts to determine similarities and differences. First level data analysis produced open codes that established tentative categories and properties. Recorded lists of codes were placed on initial master lists. A coding journal was initiated by way of an audit trail. This was deemed necessary as changes to original lists on the basis of similarities or differences necessitated tracking. Data from observations and documents underwent similar analysis.

Once all the data was coded, a second layer of analysis was conducted. In order to determine relationships, axial codes were developed and tentative propositions about practice emerged. The paradigm model, alongside open and axial coding of data, enhanced the search for patterns and groupings that defined practice. What followed involved further sorting and deciding on which categories and subcategories were established and which required moving and reconstructing as new perceptions, insights and understandings emerged. Selective coding secured the core and causal properties of practices of capacity building for improvement.

To ensure the findings met internal validity, external validity and reliability requirements, two sets of criteria were proposed: The trustworthiness criteria of credibility, transferability, dependability and confirmability (Guba & Lincoln, 1994, in Denzin & Lincoln, 1994) and the authenticity criteria of fairness, namely, 'ontological authenticity (enlarges personal constructions), educative authenticity (leads to improved understanding of constructions of others), catalytic authenticity (stimulates action), and tactical authenticity (empowers action)' (Guba & Lincoln, 1994, in Denzin & Lincoln, 1994, p. 114).

Trustworthiness and authenticity were addressed by rigorous application of grounded theory methods in data collection, analysis and interpretation as per the constant comparative method (Charmaz, 2003). A traditional take on 'triangulation' was also employed to ensure trustworthiness of data. Three forms of triangulation were employed: methodological triangulation with a focus on consistency of findings using different data-collection methods; data source triangulation where consistency of findings related to data gained from different sources but with the use of the same data collection tool; and analyst triangulation where participants verified early interpretations of the findings. Utilisation of grounded methods meant the data analysis itself was less prone to accusations of unreliability. The rigorous method of coding facilitated tracking of information to original text albeit interview transcripts, observational entries and/or document analysis. Lincoln and Guba (2003) confirm this as maintaining an audit trail.

REFERENCES

Administering for excellence. (1988). Report of the Taskforce to Review Education Administration. Wellington: Government Printer.

Alton-Lee, A. (2003). *Quality teaching for diverse students in schooling: Best evidence synthesis.* Wellington: Ministry of Education.

Alton-Lee, A. (2005). *Quality teaching for diverse learners: How an evidence-based approach can help.* Paper presented to ACSA Forum, Quality teachers: Quality teaching – Creating a new agenda for action by practitioners, researchers and policy makers, Melbourne, Australia.

Andrews, D., & Crowther, F. (2002). Parallel leadership: A clue to the contents of the "black box" of school reform. *The International Journal of Educational Management, 16*(4), 152-159.

Annan, B., Fa'amoe-Timoteo, E., Carpenter, V., Hucker, J., & Warren, S. (2004). *Strengthening education in Mangere and Otara outcomes report July 1999-June 2002.* Wellington: Ministry of Education

Annan, B., Lai, M. K., & Robinson, V. (2003). Teacher talk to improve teaching practices. *SET, 1,* 31-35.

Barth, R. (1990). *Improving schools from within.* San Francisco: Jossey-Bass.

Barrington, J. (1981). The politics of school government. In M. Clark (Ed.), *The politics of education in New Zealand.* Wellington: NZCER.

Beare, H., Caldwell, B. J., & Millikan, R. H. (1989). *Creating an excellent school: Some new management techniques.* London: Routledge.

Berra, Y. (2001). *When you come to a fork in the road, take it!* New York: Hyperion.

Biddluph, F., Biddulph, J., & Biddulph, C. (2003). *The complexity of community and family influenced on children's achievement in New Zealand: Best evidence synthesis.* Wellington: Ministry of Education.

Bolman, R., McMahon, A., Stoll, L., Thomas, S., Wallace, M., Greenwood, A., Hawkey, K., Ingram, M., Atkinson, A., & Smith, M. (2005). *Creating and sustaining effective professional learning communities* (Research Rep. No. 637). London: DfES and University of Bristol.

Boyd, R. (1998, January). *A case study of educational change in national education administration post-Picot.* Paper presented at the NZEALS conference, Wellington, New Zealand.

Boyle, B., Lamprianou, I., & Boyle, T. (2004). A longitudinal study of teacher change: What makes professional development effective? Report of the second year of the study. *School Effectiveness and School Improvement, 16*(1), 1-27.

Busher, H. (2006). *Understanding educational leadership. People, power and culture.* England: Open University Press.

Charmaz, K. (2003). Grounded theory: Objectivist and constructivist methods. In N. Denzin & Y. Lincoln (Eds.), *Strategies of qualitative inquiry* (2nd ed., pp. 249-292). Thousand Oaks, CA: Sage.

Coburn, C. (2003). Rethinking scale: Moving beyond numbers to deep and lasting change. *Educational Researcher, 32*(6), 3-12.

Codd, J. (1990). Managerialism: The problem with today's schools. *Delta, 44,* 17-25.

Codd, J. (2005). Teachers as 'managed professionals' in the global education industry: The New Zealand Experience. *Educational Review, 57*(2), 193-206.

Codd, J., Brown, M., Clark, J., Mcpherson, J., O'Neill H., O'Neill, J., Waitere-Ang, H., & Zepke, N. (2005). *Review of future-focused research on teaching and learning.* Wellington: Ministry of Education.

Connell, R. W. (1985). *Teachers' work.* Sydney, Australia: George Allen & Unwin.

Copland, M. (2003). Leadership of inquiry: Building and sustaining capacity for school improvement. *Educational Evaluation and Policy Analysis, 25*(5), 375-395.

Daft, R. L. (2002). *The leadership experience* (2nd ed.). Australia: Thomson South-Western.

Dalin, P. (2005). *School development. Theories and strategies.* London: Continuum.

Dantley, M. E. (2005). Moral leadership: Shifting the Management Paradigm. In F. W. English (Ed.), *The Sage handbook of educational leadership. Advances in theory, research, and practice* (pp. 34-47). Thousand Oaks: Sage.

Darling Hammond, L. (1996). The quiet revolution: Rethinking teacher development. *Educational Leadership, 53*(6), 4-10.

Day, C. (2000). Beyond transformational leadership. *Educational Leadership*, April, 56-59.

Day, C. (2007). Sustaining the turnaround: What capacity building means in practice. *International Symposium for Electronic Arts, 32*(3), 39-48.

Day, C., & Sachs, J. (2004). Professionalism, performativity and empowerment: Discourses in the politics, policies and purposes of continuing professional development. In C. Day & J. Sachs (Eds.), *International handbook on the professional development of teachers* (pp. 3-32). Buckingham: Open University Press.

Deal, T., & Kennedy, A. (1983). Culture and school performance. *Educational Leadership, 40*(5), 140-141.

Deal, T., & Kennedy, A. (1982). *Corporate cultures. The rites of rituals of corporate life.* London: Penguin Books.

Denzin, N. K., & Lincoln, Y. S. (1994). *Handbook of qualitative research.* Thousand Oaks, CA: Sage.

Driscoll, M. E., & Goldring, E. B. (2005). How can school leaders incorporate communities as contexts for student learning? In W. A. Firestone & Riehl (Eds.), *A new agenda for research in educational leadership* (pp. 61-80). New York: Teachers College Press.

Duncombe, R., & Armour, K. M. (2004). Collaborative professional learning: From theory to practice. *Journal of Inservice Education, 30*(1), 141-163.

Earl, L., & Lee, L. (1998). *Evaluation of the Manitoba School Improvement Programme.* Unpublished paper. Proactive Information Services Limited.

Education Review Office. (1996). *Improving schooling in Mangere and Otara.* Retrieved May 24, 2005, from http://www.ero.govt.nz.

Education Review Office. (1999). *School governance and student achievement.* Retrieved January 2, 2007, from http://www.ero.govt.nz.

Education Review Office. (2000). *Multi cultural schools in New Zealand.* Retrieved January 2, 2007, from http://www.ero.govt.nz.

Education Review Office. (2005). *Confirmed education review report* (school name withheld to maintain anonymity) Retrieved January 2, 2007, from http://www.ero.govt.nz.

Education Review Office. (2006a). *Framework for school reviews.* Retrieved January 2, 2007, from http://www.ero.govt.nz.

Education Review Office. (2006b). *The achievement of Pacific students.* Retrieved January 2, 2007, from http://www.ero.govt.nz.

Elmore, R. (1995). Structural reform and educational practice. *Educational Researcher, 24*(9), 23-26.

Elmore, R. (2002). *Bridging the gap between standards and achievement. The imperative for professional development in education.* Albert Shanker Institute. Retrieved June 12, 2003 from World Wide Web http://www.albertshanker.org/Do.

Evans-Andris, M. (2010). *Changing for good. Sustaining school improvement.* Thousand Oaks, CA: Sage.

Farquhar, S. (2003). *Quality teaching – Early foundations: Best evidence synthesis.* Wellington: Ministry of Education.

Fitzgerald, T., & Gunter, H. M. (2006) Teacher leadership: A new form of managerialism? *New Zealand journal of Educational Leadership, 21*(2), 43-56.

Fullan, M., & Mascall, B. (2000). *Human resources issues in education: A literature review.* Final report to the New Zealand Ministry of Education. Wellington: Ministry of Education.

Fullan, M. (1991). *The new meaning of educational change.* London: Cassell.

Fullan, M. (1993). *Changing forces: Probing the depths of educational reform.* London: Falmer Press.

Fullan, M. (2002). The change leader. *Educational Leadership, 59*(8), 16-20.

Fullan, M. (2005). *Leadership & sustainability. System thinkers in action.* Thousand Oaks, CA: Corwin Press.

Furman, G. C., & Shields, C. M. (2005). How can educational leaders promote and support social justice and democratic community in schools? In W. A. Firestone & Riehl (Eds.), *A new agenda for research in educational leadership* (pp. 119-137). New York: Teachers College Press.

Giles, C. (2007). Building capacity in challenging US schools: An exploration of successful leadership practice in relation to organizational learning. *International Symposium for Electronic Arts, 35*(3), 30-38.

Glaser, B. G. (1978). *Theoretical sensitivity.* Mill Valley, CA: Sociology Press.

Glaser, B. G., & Strauss, A. L. (1967). *The discovery of grounded theory: Strategies for qualitative research.* New York: Aldine De Gruyter.

Gold, E., Simon, E., & Brown, C. (2005). A new conception of parent engagement. Community organizing for school reform. In F. W. English (Ed.), *The Sage handbook of educational leadership. Advances in theory, research, and practice* (pp. 237-268). Thousand Oaks: Sage.

Goodman, J., Baron, D., & Myers, C. (2005). Constructing a democratic foundation for school-based reform. In F. W. English (Ed.), *The Sage handbook of educational leadership. Advances in theory, research, and practice* (pp. 297-331). Thousand Oaks: Sage.

Gorinski, R., & Fraser, C. (2006). *Literature review on the effective engagement of Pasifika Parents & Communities in Education (PISCPL).* Wellington: Ministry of Education.

Gronn, P. (2002). Distributed leadership as a unit of analysis. *The Leadership Quarterly, 13*(4), 423-451.

Guba, E. G., & Lincoln, Y. S. (1994). Competing paradigms in qualitative research. In N. K. Denzin and Y. S. Lincoln (Eds.), *Handbook of qualitative research* (pp. 105-117). Thousand Oaks, CA: Sage.

Hadfield, M., Chapman, C., Curryer, I., & Barrett, P. (2004). *Building capacity developing your school.* Retrieved January 20, 2004, from http://www.ncsl.org.uk.

Hallinger, P., & Snidvongs, K. (2005). *Adding value to school leadership and management. A review of trends in the development of managers in education and business sectors.* Paper commissioned for the national College for School Leadership, Nottingham, England.

Harris, A. (2003). Behind the classroom door: The challenge of organisational and pedagogical change. *Journal of Educational Change, 4,* 369-382.

Harris, A. (2004). Distributed leadership and school improvement leading or misleading? *Educational Management Administration & Leadership, 32*(1), 11-24.

Harris, A. (2010). Leading system transformation. *School Leadership and Management, 30*(3), 197-207.

Harris, A., & Lambert, L. (2003). *Building leadership capacity for school improvement.* Milton Keynes: Open University.

Harris, A., & Young, J. (2000). Comparing school improvement programmes in England and Canada. *School Leadership & Management, 20*(1), 31-40.

Hargreaves, A. (1994). *Changing teachers, changing times: Teachers' work and culture in the postmodern age.* London: Cassell.

Hargreaves, A. (1995). Cultures of teaching: A focus for change. In A. Hargreaves, & M. Fullan (Eds.), *Understanding teacher development.* London: Cassell.

Hargreaves, A., & Fink, D. (2006). The ripple effect. *Educational Leadership, 63*(8), 3-21.

Hawk, K., & Hill. J. (1997). *Towards making achieving cool. Some policy implications for student achievement in low decile schools.* Paper presented at the NZARE Conference, New Zealand.

Helu-Thaman, K. (2003). Decolonizing Pacific studies: Indigenous perspectives, knowledge, and wisdom in higher education. *The Contemporary Pacific, 15*(1), 1-17.

Hopkins, D. (1987). *Improving the quality of schooling.* Lewes: Falmer Press.

Hopkins, D. (2001). *School improvement for real.* London: Falmer Press.

Hopkins, D., Ainscow, M., & West, M. (1994). *School improvement in an era of change.* London: Cassell.

REFERENCES

Hopkins, D., Beresford, J., & West, M. (1998). Creating the conditions for classroom and teacher development. *Teachers and Teaching: Theory and Practice, 4*(1), 115-141.

Honig, M., & Hatch, T. (2004). Crafting coherence: How schools strategically manage multiple, external demands. *Educational Researcher, 33*(8), 16-30.

Kilgore, D. (1999). Understanding learning in social movements: A theory of collective learning. *International Journal of Lifelong Education, 18*(3), 191-202.

Knight, N. (2003). Teacher feedback to students in numeracy lessons: Are students getting good value? *SET, 3*, 40-45.

Lam, Y. L. J., & Punch, K. F. (2001). External environment and school organisational learning: Conceptualising the empirically neglected. *Leadership and Learning, 29*(3), 28-39.

Lange, D. (1988). *Tomorrow's schools.* Wellington: New Zealand Government Printer.

Leithwood, K. (2001). School leadership in the context of accountability policies. *Leadership in Education, 4*(3), 217-235.

Leithwood, K., & Jantzi, D. (1999). 'Transformational school leadership effects'. *School Effectiveness and School Improvement, 10*(4), 451-479.

Levin, B. (2001). *Reforming education: From origins to outcomes.* London: Routledge Falmer.

Lincoln, Y. S., & Guba, E. G. (2003). The failure of positivist science. In Y. Lincoln & N. Denzin (Eds.), *Turning points in qualitative research. Tying knots in a handkerchief* (pp. 219-239). Walnut Creek, CA: AltaMira Press.

Lindsey, R. B., Roberts, L. M., & CampbellJones, F. (2005). *The culturally proficient school. An implementation guide for school leaders.* Thousand Oaks, CA: Corwin Press.

Maden, M. (Ed.). (2001). *Success against the odds – Five years on: Revisiting effective schools in disadvantaged areas.* London: Routledge Falmer.

Marks, H. M. & Louis, K. S. (1999). Teacher empowerment and the capacity for organizational learning. *Educational Administration Quarterly, 35* (supplemental), 707-750.

McCauley, L., & Roddick, R. (2001). *An evaluation of schools support.* Wellington: Ministry of Education.

Ministry of Education. (1993a). The national education guidelines. *The Education Gazette, 72*(7), 1993.

Ministry of Education. (1993b). *The New Zealand curriculum framework.* Wellington: Ministry of Education.

Ministry of Education. (1999a). *Briefing for the incoming Minister of Education.* Wellington: Ministry of Education.

Ministry of Education. (1999b). *Professional standards: Criteria for quality teaching secondary school teachers and unit holders.* Wellington: Ministry of Education.

Ministry of Education. (2000). *Sharpening the focus.* Wellington: Learning Media.

Ministry of Education. (2004). *Statement of intent – 2003-2008.* Retrieved September 9, 2005, from http://www.minedu.govt.nz.

Ministry of Education. (2005). *Strengthening education in Mangere and Otara.* Wellington: Ministry of Education.

Ministry of Education. (2006). *Statement of Intent – 2005-2010.* Retrieved January 6, 2007, from http://www.minedu.govt.nz.

Mitchell, C., & Sackney, L. (2000). *Profound improvement: Building capacity for a learning community.* Lisse, the Netherlands: Swets and Zeitlinger.

Mitchell, L., Cameron, M., & Wylie, C. (2002). *Sustaining school improvement: Ten primary school's journeys.* Wellington: NZCER.

Mitchell, M., & Cubey, P. (2003). *Characteristics of professional development linked to enhanced pedagogy and children's learning and early childhood settings: Best evidence synthesis.* Wellington: Ministry of Education.

Mulford, D. Silins, H., & Andrew, R. (2003, November). *Leadership for organisational learning and improved student outcomes.* Paper presented for AARE/NZARE Conference, Auckland, New Zealand.

Muijs, D., & Harris, A. (2003). Teacher leadership: A review of the literature. *Educational Management & Administration, 31*(4), 437-449.

Nias, J., Southworth, G., & Yeomans, R. (1989). *Staff relationships in the primary school: A study of organisational cultures.* London: Cassell.

Nechyba, T., McEwan, P., Older-Aguilar, D. (2005). *The impact of family and community resources on student outcomes: An assessment of the international literature with implications for New Zealand.* Wellington: Ministry of Education.

New Zealand Government. (1989). Education Act, sections 60A, 61, 63 and 69.

New Zealand Government. (2001). Education Standards Act.

Northouse, P. G. (2004). *Leadership theory and practice.* Thousand Oaks, CA: Sage.

Owens, R. G. (1991). *Organisational behaviour in education* (4th ed.). Boston: Allyn and Bacon.

Patton, M. Q. (1990). *Qualitative evaluation and research methods* (2nd ed.). Newbury Park: Sage.

Phillips, G., McNaughton, S., & MacDonald, S. (2001). *Picking up the pace: Effective literacy interventions for accelerated progress over the transition into decile 1 schools. Final report to the Ministry of Education on the Professional Development associated with the Early Childhood Primary Links via Literacy (ECPL) Project.* Auckland: The Child Literacy Foundation and the Woolf Fisher Research Centre.

Potter, D., Reynolds, D., & Chapman, C. (2002). School improvement for schools facing challenging circumstances: A review of research and practice. *School Leadership and Management, 22*(3), 243-256.

Pristine, N. A., & Nelson, B. S. (2005). How can educational leaders support and promote teaching and learning? New conceptions of learning and leading in schools. In W. A. Firestone & C. Riehl (Eds.), *A new agenda for research in educational leadership* (pp. 46-61). New York: Teachers College Press.

Rae, K. (2005). More busy-work for schools. *New Zealand Journal of Educational Leadership, 20*(1), 95-97.

Raudenbush, S. (2005). Learning from attempts to improve schooling: The contribution of methodological diversity. *Research News and Comment,* June/July, 25-31.

Reynolds, D. (1999). School effectiveness, school improvement and contemporary educational policies. In J. Demaine (Ed.), *Contemporary Educational Policy and Politics.* London: MacMillan.

Reynolds, D., Hopkins, D., & Stoll, L. (1993). Linking school effectiveness knowledge and school improvement practice: Towards a synergy. *School Effectiveness and School Improvement, 4*(1), 37-58.

Robinson, V., Ward, L., Timperley, H., & Tuioti, L. (2005). *Strengthening education in Mangere and Otara: Third evaluation report.* Report to the Ministry of Education. Auckland: Auckland Uniservices Ltd.

Rosenholtz, S. (1989). *Teacher's workplace: The social organisation of schools.* New York: Teachers' College Press.

Sammons, P., Thomas, S., & Mortimer, P. (1997). *Forging links: Effective schools and effective departments.* London: Paul Chapman.

Sarason, S. (1996). *Revisiting "the culture of the school and the problem of change".* New York: Teachers College Press.

Sayles, L. R. (1964). *Managerial behaviour: Administration in complex organisations.* New York: McGraw-Hill.

Schechter, C. (2004). Teachers' perceived need to doubt: school conditions and the principal's role. *The International Journal of Educational management, 18*(3), 172-179.

Schein, E. H. (1985). *Organisational culture and leadership.* San Francisco: Jossey-Bass.

Senge, P. M. (2000). *Schools that learn.* New York: Doubleday.

Sergiovanni, T. (2006). *The principalship. A reflective practice perspective.* USA: Pearson Education, Inc.

Sharrat, L., & Fullan, M. (2009). *Realization: The change imperative for deepening district wide reform.* Ontario, CA: Corwin Press.

REFERENCES

Shields, C., & Sayani, A. (2005). Leading in the midst of diversity. The challenge of our times. In F. W. English (Ed.), *The Sage handbook of educational leadership. Advances in theory, research, and practice* (pp. 380-402). Thousand Oaks: Sage.

Slee, R., Weiner, G., & Tomlinson, S. (1998). *School effectiveness for whom?* London: Falmer Press.

Stake, R. (1994). Case studies. In N. Denzin, & Y. Lincoln (Eds.), *Handbook of qualitative research* (pp. 236-248). Thousand Oaks: Sage.

Stoll, L. (1999). School culture: Black hole or fertile garden for school improvement? In J. Prosser (Ed.), *School culture* (pp. 30-47). London: Chapman Publishing.

Stoll, L., & Fink, D. (1996). *Changing our schools. Linking school effectiveness and school improvement.* Buckingham, UK: Open University Press.

Stoll, L., Bolman, R., McMahon, A., Wallace, M., & Thomas, S. (2006). Professional learning communities: A review of the literature. *Journal of Educational Change, 7,* 221-258.

Strauss, A. (1987). *Qualitative analysis for social scientists.* New York: Cambridge University Press.

Strauss, A., & Corbin, J. (1990). *Basics of qualitative research: Grounded theory procedures and techniques.* Newbury Park, CA: Sage.

Strauss, A., & Corbin, J. (1998). *Basics of qualitative research: Techniques and procedures for developing grounded theory* (2nd ed.). Thousand Oaks, CA: Sage.

Smylie, M. A. (2010). *Continuous school improvement.* Thousand Oaks, CA: Corwin Press.

Smylie, M., Conley, S. & Marks, H. (2002). Exploring new approaches to teacher leadership for school improvement. In J. Murphy (Ed.), *The educational leadership challenge: Redefining leadership for the 21st century.* Chicago: University of Chicago Press.

Smylie, M., Wenzel, S., & Fendt, C. (2003). The Chicago Annenberg challenge: Lessons on leadership for school development. In J. Murphy & A. Datnow (Eds.), *Leadership lessons from comprehensive school reforms.* Thousand Oaks, CA: Corwin.

Symes, I., Jeffries, L., Timerley, H. S., & Lai, M. K. (2001). School's learning journeys: Evaluating a new approach to professional development in literacy at Viscount School. *SET, 2,* 3-6.

Teddlie, C., & Reynolds, D. (2000). *The international handbook of school effectiveness research.* London: Falmer.

Thrupp, M. (2001, December). *English school-level policy: Any lessons for New Zealand?* Paper presented at NZARE Conference, Christchurch, New Zealand.

Thrupp, M., & Willmott, R. (2003). *Education management in managerialist times.* Maidenhead, UK: Open University Press.

Timperley, H., & Robinson, V. (2001). Achieving schooling improvement through challenging teachers' schema. *Journal of Educational Change, 2,* 281-300.

Timperley, H., Smith, L., Parr, J., Partway, S., Mirams, S., Clark, S., Allen, M., & Page, J. (2004). *AUSAD analysis and use of student achievement data: Final evaluation report.* Report to the Ministry of Education. Auckland: Auckland Uniservices Ltd.

van Velzen, W., Miles, M., Eckholm, M., Hameyer, U., & Robinson, D. (1985). *Making school improvement work.* Leuven: ACCO.

Weller, L. D., Hartley, S. H., & Brown, C. L. (1994). Principals and TQM: Developing vision. *The Clearing House, 67*(5), 298-301.

West, M., Jackson, D., Harris, A., & Hopkins, D. (2000) Learning through leadership, leadership through learning: Leadership for sustained school improvement. In K. A. Riley & K. S. Louis (Eds.), *Leadership for change and school reform: International perspectives* (pp 30-49). London: Routledge Falmer.

Wenger, E., McDermott, R., & Snyder, W. M. (2002). *Cultivating communities of practice.* USA: Harvard Business School Press.

Whitty, G., Power, S., & Haplin, T. (1998). *Devolution and choice in education: The school, the state, and the market.* Buckingham, UK: Open University Press.

Yin, R. K. (2003). *Case study research: Design and methods* (3rd ed.). Thousand Oaks, CA: Sage.

York-Barr, J., & Duke, K. (2004). What do we know about teacher leadership? Findings from two decades of scholarship. *Review of Educational Research, 74*(3), 255-315.

CPSIA information can be obtained at www.ICGtesting.com
Printed in the USA
BVOW04s1332160913

331298BV00002B/31/P

9 789462 093270